CONTENTS

	Abbreviations and Acronyms	2
	Acknowledgements	2
	Notes	2
	Introduction	3
1	Kings of Battle: Western Artillery Guns	4
2	L119 & M777: Lightweight Champions	5
3	M109: Long-lived Paladin	17
4	Panzerhaubitze 2000: The Gold Standard	25
5	AS90 & *Krab*: A Marriage of Convenience	34
6	CAESAR: Way of the Future?	42
7	The Dana Family: Warsaw Pact to NATO	49
	Appendix: Projectiles	57
	Selected Bibliography	59
	Endnotes	60
	About the Author	64

Helion & Company Limited
Unit 8 Amherst Business Centre
Budbrooke Road
Warwick
CV34 5WE
England
Tel. 01926 499 619
Email: info@helion.co.uk
Website: www.helion.co.uk
Twitter: @helionbooks
https://helionbooks.wordpress.com/

Text © Wen-Jian Chung 2025
Photographs © as individually credited
Colour profiles © David Bocquelet 2025

Cover image: Ukrainian M777 firing at Russian forces, May 2022. (MOU)

Designed and typeset by Mach 3 Solutions (www.mach3solutions.co.uk)
Cover design Paul Hewitt, Battlefield Design (www.battlefield-design.co.uk)

Every reasonable effort has been made to trace copyright holders and to obtain their permission for the use of copyright material. The author and publisher apologise for any errors or omissions in this work, and would be grateful if notified of any corrections that should be incorporated in future reprints or editions of this book.

ISBN: 978-1-804517-23-9

British Library Cataloguing-in-Publication Data
A catalogue record for this book is available from the British Library

All rights reserved. No part of this publication may be reproduced, stored in a retrieval system, or transmitted, in any form, or by any means, electronic, mechanical, photocopying, recording or otherwise, without the express written consent of Helion & Company Limited.

We always welcome receiving book proposals from prospective authors.

Note: In order to simplify the use of this book, all names, locations and geographic designations are as provided in *The Times World Atlas*, or other traditionally accepted major sources of reference, as of the time of described events.

ABBREVIATIONS AND ACRONYMS

AAMG	anti-aircraft machine gun	**MOU**	*Minoborony Ukrainy* (Ukrainian Ministry of Defence)
AFV	armoured fighting vehicle		
APU	auxiliary power unit	**MRSI**	multiple rounds simultaneous impact
AT	anti-tank	**NBC**	nuclear, biological, and chemical
BB	base bleed	**NHU**	*Natsionalna hvardiia Ukrainy* (National Guard of Ukraine)
BMS	battlefield management system		
DPICM	dual-purpose improved conventional munition	**PGM**	precision-guided munition
ERA	explosive reactive armour	**RAP**	rocket-assisted projectile
FCS	fire control system	**RHA**	rolled homogeneous armour
FPV	first-person view drone	**ROK**	Republic of Korea, colloquially South Korea
GPS	Global Positioning System	**SNS**	satellite navigation system
JBMoU	Joint Ballistics Memorandum of Understanding	**SP**	self-propelled
MBT	main battle tank	**SPG**	self-propelled gun
MG	machine gun	**UAS**	uncrewed aerial system, colloquially 'drone'
MoD	Ministry of Defence (UK, unless otherwise specified)	**ZSU**	*Zbroyini syly Ukrainy* (Armed Forces of Ukraine)

ACKNOWLEDGEMENTS

The author wishes to thank: his NHU artilleryman acquaintance in Ukraine (who wishes to remain anonymous) for giving insight into how artillery is used on the battlefield and his experiences with *Giatsint*-B and other pieces; Antoni Walkowski for discussions about the history of the *Krab* SPG; Steph ('Praise The Steph' on BlueSky and Twitter) for discussions about the *Dana* SPG family; CJ ('Casual Arty Fan' on Twitter) for some insights into US artillery doctrine and his experience with the M119; @prekrasnii1 on Twitter, a currently serving Ukrainian M109A6 Paladin gunner in the 47th Mechanised Brigade, for his willingness to be interviewed; Arsenii Gerasimenko for his kind permission in using his photos of the 43rd Artillery Brigade's PzH 2000s; Petr P. of Guerilla Medicine for kindly allowing use of his *Zuzana* 2 photo (a rarely photographed piece in Ukraine).

The author also wishes to thank Tom Cooper and David Bocquelet for their tremendous support in making this book a reality.

The appearance of US Department of Defense (DoD) visual information does not imply or constitute DoD endorsement.

NOTES

In addition to the barrel bore diameter (i.e. calibre), Western artillery guns are also often distinguished by the length of the barrel in calibres. Example: the M777 howitzer is often described as a '155mm L/39' howitzer, indicating that it has a bore diameter of 155mm and a barrel length of approximately 6.1m (39 calibres i.e. 155 x 39mm). The author will adopt this shorthand generally to describe gun barrel length. Unless otherwise noted, this length does not include the muzzle brake.

Figures for shell velocities refer to the muzzle velocity. Due to air resistance and the laws of ballistics, shells will slow down in flight.

Soviet, Russian, and Ukrainian engines are rated in metric horsepower (1hp = 0.735kW). This is different to the imperial/mechanical horsepower commonly used in the US (1hp = 0.745kW). For consistency, metric horsepower will be used throughout the book.

For Soviet-designed artillery pieces, the emplacement/displacement time, i.e. time to bring a gun into/out of action, is provided as given in the manual. This time does not include the artillery survey time for laying the guns or preparing ammunition, which is included in Western emplacement time figures, thus they cannot be directly compared.

In the 'Context' sections, it will often be said that '[system] was intended for [purpose] in [unit type]'. It is very important to remember that, in practice, the distribution and use of these systems can vary significantly from the original intention, especially during wartime. Thus, these statements should be taken only as a general rule-of-thumb.

The numbers of Western artillery pieces donated to Ukraine are taken from the Oryx Blog (oryxspioenkop.com/2022/04/answering-call-heavy-weaponry-supplied.html), unless otherwise noted. It should be noted that not all aid is publicly announced.

Statistics for losses of the Armed Forces of the Russian Federation (oryxspioenkop.com/2022/02/attack-on-europe-documenting-equipment.html) and of the Armed Forces of Ukraine (oryxspioenkop.com/2022/02/attack-on-europe-documenting-ukrainian.html) are taken from the Oryx Blog, which keeps a tally of visible losses. These numbers are likely to be underestimates, as artillery usually operates farther from the frontlines and there is less likely to be visual evidence of its loss.

As a final note, in the technical summaries, the radios and other communications equipment are listed as given in manuals or books, where available. However, this equipment may be considered sensitive by Western militaries and some are removed before being sent to Ukraine, replaced by other equipment such as the ubiquitous Motorola radios commonly found in Ukrainian vehicles.

INTRODUCTION

> *In battle, the artillery has always had two roles. In defence, its purpose is to destroy the impetus of the enemy's attacks, and in attack, its task is to destroy the enemy's will to resist. Just that. And whether you consider the medieval wars or the Napoleonic wars or the great wars that followed them, those two tasks have remained.*
> — General Sir Thomas Lovett Morony, KCB, OBE, Master Gunner, St James's Park (1985)[1]

War is ultimately the infliction of violence on the enemy in pursuit of political goals. This is as true today as it was in the thirteenth century, when the Chinese invented gunpowder cannons. There are only two ways for a land army to inflict violence: direct or indirect fires. A modern army's infantry and armour are its primary direct-fire instruments, its 'melee' weapons in a sense. Artillery is traditionally the army's primary organic means for indirect fire, flinging explosives at the enemy. New weapons such as armed first-person view (FPV) drones have recently appeared to challenge the dominance of artillery in this role. However, when it comes to efficiently and reliably inflicting violence in the worst of conditions, the brutal simplicity of an artillery gun firing an explosive shell is hard to beat.

In the twenty-first century, as Russia seeks to reclaim its 'rightful' status as a great power, it has attempted to subjugate independent Ukraine under its dominion. Russia's annexation of Crimea in 2014 marked the beginning of the Russo-Ukrainian War, the largest conventional war in Europe since 1945. What started off as a hybrid war of plausible deniability in the Donbas would escalate into a full-scale invasion in 2022 that continues to this day, over 10 years after the Crimean annexation. However, what has not changed since 2014 is the dominant role that the artillery has played on the battlefield for both sides.

Ukraine inherited a considerable artillery arm from the USSR. However, while Soviet-legacy gun artillery systems played a key role in blunting the initial stages of the 2022 invasion, they have since been supplemented or replaced by Western towed and self-propelled guns (SPGs) as wear and combat losses have attrited their numbers. Though relatively small in number on paper, these systems, which are arguably qualitatively superior to Soviet-legacy systems, have also played a critical role in the Ukrainian defence. Ukraine has also seen its artillery doctrine shift away from Soviet-style massed fires towards one that emphasises precision and artillery as a force multiplier more in alignment with Western military ideas.

Despite the critical role gun artillery has played and continues to play in the Russo-Ukrainian War, the technical aspects and histories of the individual artillery systems used by both sides have received relatively little attention in English. They are often lumped together as generic 'artillery', which is understandable: unlike fighter planes or, to a lesser extent, tanks and other vehicles, to most people an artillery gun is not very different from another one. The goal of this book is to attempt to shed more light on what makes each system special in its own way and how it contributes to this artillery-dominated war that continues to rage on at the time of writing.

This book is the second volume of a two-book 'guide' to major gun artillery pieces in use during the Russo-Ukrainian War and focuses on Western and domestic designs used by Ukraine. Although each system's chapter is self-contained, the author recommends reading the first book for a primer on artillery fire control.

Regrettably, due to the extraordinary variety of systems currently in use, the author will only be able to cover some of the more important ones in detail. This is especially true for the systems donated by Ukraine's allies, which form a veritable zoo that cannot hope to be completely covered in two books of this length. This book will also not cover infantry mortars, as these are generally operated by infantrymen and are not usually found within artillery units, nor will it cover rocket artillery or tactical ballistic missiles; they would need their own volumes to describe adequately.

Ukrainian crew trains on a Norwegian M109A3GN at the Grafenwoehr training range in Germany, May 2022. These were among the first SPGs sent by the West as aid to Ukraine. (DoD)

1
KINGS OF BATTLE: WESTERN ARTILLERY GUNS

The US Army refers to artillery as the 'King of Battle': by the end of the Second World War its Field Artillery branch had proved itself fully deserving that moniker, with British historian and artillery officer Shelford Bidwell describing them 'second to none in efficiency'.[1] The British Royal Artillery were themselves no slouches, described by Swedish artillery officer and historian Stig Moberg as a 'thoroughly efficient arm, able to deliver concentrations of the heaviest fire in support of the infantry and armour, both day and night'.[2] Both the US and UK fielded some truly outstanding artillery pieces during the war; these, their doctrines, and the new enemy they faced across the Iron Curtain during the Cold War would largely determine the equipment the new NATO coalition would subsequently develop.

Western Cold War artillery designs had to take into account the assumption that they would be severely outnumbered by their Soviet counterparts. This was expounded most eloquently in a 1951 article in *Combat Forces Journal*:

We face a contest where the edge our artillery may enjoy in professional excellence could be wholly blunted by inferiority in numbers...It is not enough for American artillery to be faster and more flexible than our enemy when...his infantry, artillery, and armor can smother us by sheer number. To answer this challenge we must develop more fire power per artilleryman.[3]

American gunners of 'C' Battery, 90th Field Artillery Battalion, 25th Infantry Division lay down a 'murderous barrage' with a 155mm Howitzer M1 (postwar, M114) on Japanese artillery positions in Balete Pass, Luzon, Philippines. Ukraine has received some M114s from Portugal and Greece, but there are no known photos of it in Ukrainian service. (NARA)

Written during the Korean War, where United Nations forces faced massed attacks from the Soviet-backed Communist Korean People's Army and Chinese People's Volunteer Army employing infiltration and penetration tactics, these experiences left a great impression. The quest for 'more firepower per artilleryman' has usually led to a greater willingness in the West to introduce advanced features such as automated fire control, automatic loading, auxiliary propulsion units (APUs) for towed artillery, and other qualitative improvements. It also led to an emphasis on mechanisation and the adoption of fully enclosed 360° traverse turreted SPGs. Best exemplified by the ubiquitous American M109, which set the standard for Cold War Western SPG design, their enhanced mobility allowed for more efficient massing of fires and keeping up with armoured and mechanised units as well as greater survivability on a potentially nuclear battlefield. The threat of enemy penetration, infiltration, and envelopment, as the North Koreans and Chinese had done, meant that flanks and rear areas were more vulnerable than before, thus 360° traverse was needed to be able to respond and protect against such threats.[4]

The post-Cold War world, as a part of the so-called 'peace dividend' and the greater focus placed on counterinsurgency and counterterrorism operations, has generally resulted in less Western investment in the development of traditional tracked SPGs for high-intensity warfare. With less money to go around and a greater emphasis on expeditionary warfare, cheaper alternatives have emerged in the form of wheeled or truck-mounted SPGs, the foremost example of which is the French CAESAR. However, it has also seen the entrance of new players in the field of Western SPG development. One of these is the Republic of Korea (ROK), whose rapidly developing arms industry has experienced unprecedented success with the K9 Thunder on the export market, unseen since the M109. Another is Poland, whose *Krab* SPG (based on technology from the Korean K9 and British AS90) is currently playing a major role in the Ukrainian artillery arm.

NATO military doctrine stresses also interoperability and much equipment is standardised via STANAG and other agreements: standard NATO field artillery calibres are 105mm and 155mm. Most 155mm systems described here were designed according to the technical annexes of the Joint Ballistics Memorandum of Understanding (JBMoU) between France, Germany, Italy, the UK, and the US, which has since become the manufacturing standard for 155mm guns and ammunition around the world.[5] It stipulates some of the following requirements for L/39 and L/52 barrels:

- L/39: fire standard 43.5kg L15A1 shell or equivalent with five DM92 modular charges (or equivalent) at 810m/s, achieving 24km range under standard conditions.
- L/52: fire the same shell with six DM92 modular charges (or equivalent) at 945m/s, achieving 30km range under standard conditions. With extended-range shells, in excess of 40km.[6]

As such, in terms of range and ammunition compatibility, L/39 and L/52 guns are for most intents and purposes identical within those categories. However, not all the NATO 155mm systems and ammunition are identical: they differ enough in terms of ballistics that this must be accounted for in the fire control calculations.

The 2022 full-scale Russian invasion has shattered the pervasive complacency that much of the Western world had over the future prospects for high-intensity warfare and the artillery's role. Often dismissed as obsolete in a world of precision-guided munitions (PGMs), missiles, airpower, and unmanned/uncrewed aerial systems (UASs), combat experience from the Russo-Ukrainian War has shown that the 'King of Battle' is just as important for modern militaries in peer warfare today as it was for Napoleon over 200 years ago. Since February 2022, Ukraine has received or bought a wide variety of artillery systems from the US and other Western NATO allies. As Ukraine's Soviet-legacy artillery is worn down from attrition and the Soviet ammunition stocks dwindle, the importance of NATO and Western-supplied systems will only grow as time passes. Europe and the USA are rejuvenating long-neglected production capacities for artillery and ammunition to both arm Ukraine and themselves in the face of the post-2022 geopolitical reality, racing against the Russian military-industrial complex. The question is if they will do so fast enough to allow the Ukrainian artillery arm to attain a decisive advantage over its Russian opponents.

At the time of writing, the US has not yet made the transition to the longer L/52 barrel, and its primary 155mm systems, the M777A2 and M109A6, still use L/39 barrels. The major European nations have moved to the L/52, while the latest Ukrainian-produced artillery system, *Bohdana*, is also based around it. It is probable that in the long term Ukraine will transition completely to the 155mm calibre and phase out 152mm systems entirely, although this is unlikely to happen while the nation is still at war. In a November 2024 interview with RBC-Ukraine, the ZSU's (*Zbroyini syly Ukrainy*, Armed Forces of Ukraine) Deputy Commander of Missile Forces and Artillery, Colonel Serhiy Musienko, noted that Ukraine now uses 155mm systems the most, followed by 122mm, 105mm, and then 152mm. He further stated that the ratio of 152mm to 155mm ammunition expenditure is 1:10.[7]

2
L119 & M777: LIGHTWEIGHT CHAMPIONS

105mm L119/M119

Development History

The Great War fundamentally reshaped the British Army's attitude towards artillery and its usage on the battlefield after 1918, placing great importance on two things: 'economy of firepower' and 'mobility of firepower'. British doctrine saw the field artillery's primary goal as *neutralisation*: preventing enemy movement and observation, and the effective use of weapons, thus suppressing enemy forces and helping the supported arm (infantry/armour) to achieve its objectives. The actual destruction of men and materiel, while desirable, was not necessarily the objective, unlike in American doctrine. By concentrating their fires, this would allow for maximum effect with the given means ('economy of firepower').

The British were also obsessed with speed when responding to calls for fire, thus the ability to concentrate firepower when and where it was needed without re-deploying the guns was considered highly valuable ('mobility of firepower').[1]

These two factors strongly influenced the design of the Ordnance QF ('quick-firing') 25-pounder field gun, the workhorse artillery piece of the British Commonwealth forces during the Second World War. This was an 88mm L/28 weapon that could fire an 11.5kg (25lb, hence '25-pounder') shell out to 12.2km. It had a maximum rate-of-fire of six to eight rounds/minute and could sustain up to five during intense bombardments. The shell was lighter than its German or American 105mm counterparts, but was more than sufficient for neutralisation. Its carriage also featured a circular firing platform: when emplaced, the gun's wheels were transferred on to the platform, allowing it to be quickly traversed through 360° using the wheels. Thus, it could be rapidly aimed in any direction without having to displace the gun.[2]

The 1950s and 1960s marked a period of great transition for the British military, as it transformed from a large conscript army into a smaller professional army Garrington Ltd. began developing the 88mm X5E1 as a replacement for the 25-pounder. This highly unusual-looking weapon retained the circular firing platform and had an upswept trail and overhead dome-like shield to protect the crew against nuclear flash and shrapnel, but was abandoned in 1958 after serious flaws were discovered in the design and NATO adopted 105mm as a standard calibre.[3] The 1956 Suez debacle had, among other things, also revealed a need for something more powerful than the American 75mm Pack Howitzer M1 to equip its airmobile brigades. As a result, the British adopted the Italian 105/14 M56 pack howitzer as the L5 Pack Howitzer to equip these units in 1959.[4]

L119 Light Gun in service with the 79th Tavrian Air Assault Brigade, May 2024. Designed for use by airborne forces, its airliftable/air-droppable capability is not used in Ukraine, as the relatively static nature of the war and lack of air superiority precludes large-scale air assaults by either side. (ArmyTV)

Dutch QF 25-pounder seen during the Indonesian War of Independence in Java, Indonesia, March 1949. The circular firing platform is clearly visible. The 25-pounder remains in service with a few countries today. (Nationaal Archief)

The M56 (also often called the OTO Melara Mod. 56 or simply 'Melara' after its manufacturer) was originally designed for the Italian Alpini mountain troops. Its light weight (under 1.3t) made it a popular choice for militaries to equip light artillery units, and it has seen combat in multiple wars, including the Russo-Ukrainian War. It can also fire the very common American 105mm M1 family of ammunition originally developed for the Second World War-vintage 105mm M101 howitzer (which is also used by Ukraine today), though the short L/14 barrel meant it could only do so out to a maximum of 10km instead of 11.2km for the M101.[5] The author's NHU acquaintance has personal experience with it:

> The Melara is a joke of an artillery piece but an excellent mortar (i.e. it's useless at anything except targeting infantry at the front, but boy does it kill them well)…nobody really likes them. The whole shtick about having to assemble the gun onsite is not fun (you really can't tow it since there's no suspension, all the bolts will get unscrewed and so on). They are also NOT durable in the mechanical sense: the parts are light and can't take the stress of high intensity firing.

British experience with the M56 does not appear to have been more positive, since almost immediately after it entered service the British began contemplating a replacement.

In 1965, General Staff Requirement 3058 for a 'Light Weight Close Support Weapon System' was formally approved, which soon changed to '105mm Light Gun'. Development was undertaken by the Royal Armament Research and Development Establishment (RARDE) at Fort Halstead, Kent. Instead of the common US M1 105mm ammunition, the RARDE opted for the '105mm Field' family of ammunition as used by the 105mm L13 gun on the British Army's new L109 Abbot (FV433) SPG. This had a different charge with an electrical primer (the M1 used percussion primers), which meant that they were not interchangeable, though this was considered more acceptable as the 105mm Field Mk. 2 ammunition was significantly more powerful and had a longer range. The final design was accepted in 1970, but the finalised L118 Light Gun with L19 ordnance did not enter service until 1976. Simultaneously, the shorter L20 ordnance using M1 ammunition was developed for the Light Gun in order to make use of the large stocks inherited from the retired L5s for training purposes. Light Guns with the L20 ordnance were designated L119 in British service.[6]

After making its successful combat debut during the Falklands War in 1982, the Light Gun would see considerable export success and was even adopted and built under licence by the US to replace its old M101 and M102 105mm howitzers. This was naturally in the L119 form as the 105mm Towed Light Howitzer M119, with the appropriate minor changes to suit American manufacturing and US Army practices.[7] The latest version in use is the M119A3, which featured changes to the gun to simplify maintenance and improve reliability, as well as the introduction of automated gun-laying (fire control) systems.[8] Australia would build both L118 and L119 versions for Australian and New Zealand use under licence: they are often known as 'Hamel Guns' after the gun trials, which were codenamed Project Hamel.[9] The Australian guns were retired in 2013: some of the L119s were sold to BAE Systems, later bought by the British government and donated to Ukraine after the 2022 invasion. The US has also donated some M119A3s to Ukraine. At the time of writing, Ukraine does not operate the L118, thus the technical summary will not cover it. For brevity, 'Light Gun' will be used to refer to the family in general.

Technical Summary

The L119 and M119 versions of the Light Gun use a 105mm L/30 monobloc barrel with a single-baffle muzzle brake that dissipates 30 percent of the recoil. Using the common M67 charges, they are capable of throwing the standard 16kg M1 HE shell at just under 500m/s out to 11.5km. The US has also developed extended-range ammunition such as M927 RAP (rocket-assisted projectile), which has a range of up to 19km and is known to be used by the Ukrainians.[10] Ammunition is of the semi-fixed type, which means that the shell and charge are loaded as one piece, but can be separated to adjust the charges as needed. A manually-operated vertical sliding-block breech is used to save weight, allowing for a high rate-of-fire when combined with the one-piece ammunition: the BAE brochure advertises a burst rate-of-fire of 15 rounds in one minute. The barrel also has a fairly long rated life of 7,500 EFCs (equivalent full charges) and is autofrettaged to maximise strength-to-weight. The M119A3 also has some changes to the recoil system and breech to increase durability.

The L119/M119 can elevate up to 70°, which with the variable charge ammunition allows for high-arcing howitzer-like trajectories. The gun has a fine traverse of ~6° to either side, but also has effectively 360° traverse by rotating the gun's wheels on the circular platform.

Left: 105/14 M56 pack howitzer in service with one of the NHU's Omega special purpose units, July 2024. At least six were donated by Spain to Ukraine after 2022. Right: Abbot at the Abingdon Air & Country Show 2016. Roughly comparable to the Soviet *Gvozdika*, the Abbot's L13 ordnance formed the basis for the L118 Light Gun. (NHU Omega; Paul Lucas)

71st Jaeger Brigade gunner prepares to fire a 105mm M101 howitzer. The basic design of the M101 dates back to 1920, though it would not enter service as the M2A1 until 1941. Produced in vast numbers, it has been widely exported to US allies and is still in service with many countries today. Lithuania donated their M101s to Ukraine after the 2022 invasion. (71 Jaeger)

M119A3 firing at Russian forces, April 2023. In Ukrainian use, it is common for the breech operator to also act as the loader. (ArmyInform)

Some differences between the L119 with L7A1 dial sight (left) and M119A3 with M137 panoramic telescope (right) in Ukrainian service can be seen in this side-by-side comparison. Both are serving with the Ukrainian Air Assault Forces: the M119A3 belongs to the 77th Airmobile Brigade operating near Bakhmut in March 2023, while the L119's unit is unknown. The L119 gunner is using a hammer to fire the gun, most likely because of a faulty firing lever. The author has been informed by an Australian L118 ex-gunner that this is the authorised procedure for safely firing the gun without the lever. Note the DFCS mounting bracket above the barrel of the M119A3. (ArmyTV; 77 Airmobile)

This system was inherited from the 25-pounder in line with the British requirements for 'mobility of firepower', allowing it to shift fire rapidly. The gun can be fired with its wheels on the ground as well without the platform if conditions permit. For manual aiming, the L119 uses the British Hall & Watts Artillery Sighting System with L7A1 dial sight (panoramic telescope in UK parlance) developed from the Second World War German Leitz Rbl.F. 59, and it can also be fitted with a direct-fire telescopic sight.[11,12] The American M119A3 is fitted with the M137 panoramic telescope, the same type used on other towed US howitzers such as the 155mm M777. The M119A3 in American service is fitted with the Digital Fire Control System (DFCS) automated gun-laying system, which includes an inertial navigation unit, laser rangefinder, datalink, and GPS integration.[13] However, the DFCS is not fitted to earlier batches of M119A3s sent to Ukraine, though later batches would retain it. The Australian/British L119s they use also do not have automated gun-laying; thus, Ukrainian L119/M119s are aimed the old-fashioned way using their panoramic telescopes.

The Light Gun's configuration is descended from the QF 25-pr: instead of movable split trails found on most modern artillery pieces, the Light Gun's trail assembly uses two fixed curved steel tubes that join together at the end with a circular firing platform, allowing fire to be shifted quickly in any direction. This sturdy arrangement provides space for the gun to elevate and recoil into, and also reduces emplacement/displacement time, as there is no need to fold/unfold the trail. The gun carriage is made of corrosion-resistant steel, while the platform is made of aluminium and steel. With modern fire control, the gun can be emplaced/displaced within one minute; preparing to fire will take longer using only dial sights due to the need to conduct the artillery survey. The normal gun complement is a crew of six, but the gun itself can be adequately served by just three (gunner, breech operator, loader). The entire gun weighs around 1.9t and is light enough to be airlifted, air-dropped, or towed by the ubiquitous HMMWV (High Mobility Multipurpose Wheeled Vehicle, 'Humvee') 4x4 utility vehicle.

L119 'Olenka' in its folded transport configuration. The circular firing platform can be clearly seen, along with an assembled round on the right. The gun does not necessarily need to be folded for towing, and sometimes this is skipped out of expediency. (ArmyInform)

Context

In July 2022, the British government announced the transfer of 36 L119s to Ukraine.[14] This was soon followed by the US, which has provided at least 72 M119s to Ukraine at the time of writing. In preparation for this, training of Ukrainian soldiers on the L119 was conducted in the UK with the assistance of personnel from the New Zealand Army.[15] It is safe to assume that the Americans also began training Ukrainians on how to use the M119 at around this time as well, for the two guns do not share the same sights and also differ somewhat in the breech design and other aspects. By early August, the first L119s were already in action in Ukraine.[16] No L118s are known to have been provided at the time of writing, and it is unlikely they will be sent due to the relatively uncommon ammunition they use.

The Light Gun has proved to be a very successful and well-liked weapon in Ukraine. It is mostly used by the Air Assault Forces, though some mechanised brigades such as 92 Mech. are known to have also received some. The Light Gun is most comparable to the 122mm D-30 in terms of its envisaged role: in an ArmyTV interview, 'Yaroslav' of 79 Air Assault compared his L119 favourably with the D-30, praising its lightness and accuracy. When the interviewer brought up the lower range of the L119 compared to the D-30 (12km vs. 15km), 'Yaroslav' did not seem to mind, stating that he preferred to 'hit the enemy more effectively than stand further away' and that the range difference was not really significant. He noted that the lighter 105mm shell was not as effective against tanks, but their primary targets are the more common Russian infantry attacks.[17] Another advantage noted by Light Gun users in Ukraine was the low amount of flash produced by the gun when firing, a significant boon for concealment, especially at night from ever-present UAS spotters.[18] The gun is also quite small (roughly half the width and height of a D-30), which further aids concealment. The L119/M119 also benefit from the existence of more modern ammunition types than the D-30, such as the M1130 HE pre-formed fragmentation (PFF) BB (base bleed) shell with improved lethality and the M927 RAP, both of which are known to have been supplied to Ukraine. The Light Gun is also reportedly very reliable, with an 'indestructible barrel'.[19]

A significant disadvantage of the introduction of the Light Gun into Ukrainian service is the 105mm ammunition, which is not currently produced in Ukraine. The 105mm M1 family is quite commonly found around the world, but its major manufacturers are the US and ROK. While both countries have large stocks and production capacity for it, the ROK presently does not directly supply ammunition to Ukraine due to political and legal constraints, and the Republican-controlled US Congress's months-long blockade of Ukrainian aid in 2023–2024 has also shown the risks of depending on the US. However, the Light Gun is a highly capable, mobile, and reliable weapon that has proven itself well-suited to the Ukrainian battlefield. In August 2023, the Ukrainian government and BAE agreed on a partnership to produce L119s in Ukraine, indicating that Ukraine wants more of them for the foreseeable future.[20]

155mm M777

Development History

Like many countries, the American military still uses towed artillery for certain units like truck-borne motorised infantry units or expeditionary-focused ones such as the US Marine Corps (USMC) and US Army's Airborne units. This is because of their lower cost, complexity, and (especially for the latter) weight compared to SPGs. In the 1980s, the 155mm Howitzer M198 became the US Army and Marine Corps' primary towed field howitzer, replacing the long-serving Second World War-era M114. It was a fairly conventional design with split trails and a 155mm L/39 barrel weighing about 7.2t, which could be carried by the US Army and USMC's heavy-

L119 of the 46th Airmobile Brigade during the Ukrainian counteroffensive on the Zaporizhzhia front, August 2023. The loader/breech operator is eating a watermelon. Unassembled 105mm semi-fixed rounds can be seen next to the gun. (46 Airmobile)

lift helicopters, the Vertol (now Boeing) CH-47 Chinook and Sikorsky CH-53 Sea Stallion. In the mid-1980s, the US Army had sought proposals for a Lightweight Towed Howitzer Demonstrator, but this was cancelled after the US Congress cut funding, citing a lack of need.

Sensing an opportunity, the British company Vickers Shipbuilding and Engineering Ltd. (VSEL, today part of BAE) began developing the Ultra-lightweight Field Howitzer (UFH) as a private initiative. When approached, the US Army indicated its interest and encouraged VSEL to develop and submit the UFH for full evaluation. The goal was to create a weapon with performance comparable to the M198, but also weighing no more than 4t, over 40 percent lighter. However, VSEL set an even more ambitious weight target of 3.6t, allowing the UFH to be carried by the Army's standard medium-lift helicopter, the Sikorsky UH-60M Black Hawk. This would be achieved with the combination of innovative design and

M777A2 in Ukrainian service, May 2022; the unorthodox configuration of the howitzer is readily apparent. (MOU)

USMC M198 during exercises in Hawaii, USA. The barrel can be elevated past 90° to lie flat over the trails during towing to reduce length, although this has not been done in this case. Large numbers of these remain in storage in the US. (USMC, DoD)

extensive use of titanium alloys and other modern manufacturing methods in its construction.[21]

The first two prototype UFHs were completed in 1988, by which time the USMC had also become interested in the UFH. These used modified 155mm M284 barrels from the M109 SPG, made by the American Watervliet Arsenal to VSEL's specifications. Firing trials were conducted in the UK in 1989, followed by Army/USMC demonstrations the next year. Subsequently, the UFH underwent competitive trials before being selected as the XM777 Joint Lightweight 155mm Howitzer (LW155) in 1997. It was eventually accepted into service as the M777 Lightweight Howitzer, entering full-rate production in 2005.[22] The M777A1 added the DFCS upgrade similar to that already mentioned in the Light Gun section, while the M777A2 introduced the M1155 Enhanced Portable Inductive Artillery Fuze Setter (EPIAFS), allowing the howitzer to fire the M982 Excalibur GPS/INS PGM, as well as datalink capabilities.

By 2014, all US Army and USMC M777s had been brought up to the M777A2 standard, while it is also the model that was exported to Australia. Canada has also bought the M777 to equip the Royal Canadian Horse Artillery, although their model is the M777C1, which has the Digital Gun Management System (DGMS) developed by Leonardo and the Canadian Army's Land Software Engineering Centre instead of the DFCS of American M777A2s. The vast majority of the M777s supplied to Ukraine are M777A2s from the US or Australia, with only a single-digit number of M777C1s from Canada. Thus, the technical summary will focus on the M777A2.

Technical Summary

The M777A2 uses the 155mm M776 L/39 barrel, capable of throwing the standard 47kg M795 HE projectile at 802m/s out to approximately 24km at maximum charge. With the Excalibur PGM, it can attain ranges up to 40km. Since 2019, these barrels have been delivered with chrome bores for significantly improved barrel life. The barrel is capped by a double-baffle muzzle brake, which also has a towing eye similar to the Soviet D-30 howitzer and 30 percent efficiency. Unlike most Soviet (and Russian) artillery pieces, the M777 (and all other NATO 155mm pieces) uses bagged modular charges without a casing. In order to ensure proper obturation, the M777 thus has a semi-automatic interrupted screw breech. There is no mechanical rammer, but a loading tray swings the heavy projectile into the loading line to be rammed in manually with a ramrod. The manufacturer's brochure lists an 'intense' rate-of-fire of four rounds/minute for two minutes, with two rounds/minute sustained.

American and Australian M777A2s are fitted with the DFCS, which was already described in the L119/M119 Light Gun section.[23] However, as with the M119A3s, earlier batches of Ukrainian M777A2s have had most or all of the DFCS components stripped, possibly due to sensitive technology; the Ukrainians aim these M777s the 'old-fashioned' way using the M137A2 panoramic telescope.[24] However, the author has been told that later batches retain them. Because of the lack of room behind the M777, the gunner must stand to the side of the howitzer to aim it this way. Ukraine has, however, been provided with the EPIAFS, a handheld device used to feed GPS coordinates into the Excalibur PGM, thus allowing them to fire Excalibur from their M777A2s. The barrel can be elevated up 70°, with an on-mount traverse of 22.5° to either side (restricted to 19.3° if the wheels are locked down). The full crew complement for an M777 is nine personnel; however, the minimum required is only five. According to the manufacturer and the US Army, emplacement/displacement times are between two to three minutes, though there is video evidence of a Ukrainian crew accomplishing displacement in one minute and 15 seconds.[25]

Ukrainian M777A2 firing at Russian targets, May 2022. The US has not migrated to the NATO 155mm L/52 barrel: the M777A2 still has an L/39 barrel and thus a shorter range than most recent 155mm systems. (MOU)

Top: M777A2's interrupted screw breech (left) and M137A2 panoramic telescope (right). The panel next to the crewman is the gunner display associated with the DFCS. Some Ukrainian M777A2s do not have DFCS, and sometimes this panel is removed, as seen in the bottom left and centre pictures. Bottom: loading an M777A2. The silver object is the loading tray, which is used to swing projectiles into the loading line (centre). The M777's ramrod (right) is curved: since the gun is mounted so low to the ground, it would be difficult to ram the projectile in with a straight rod, especially at high elevations. (ArmyInform)

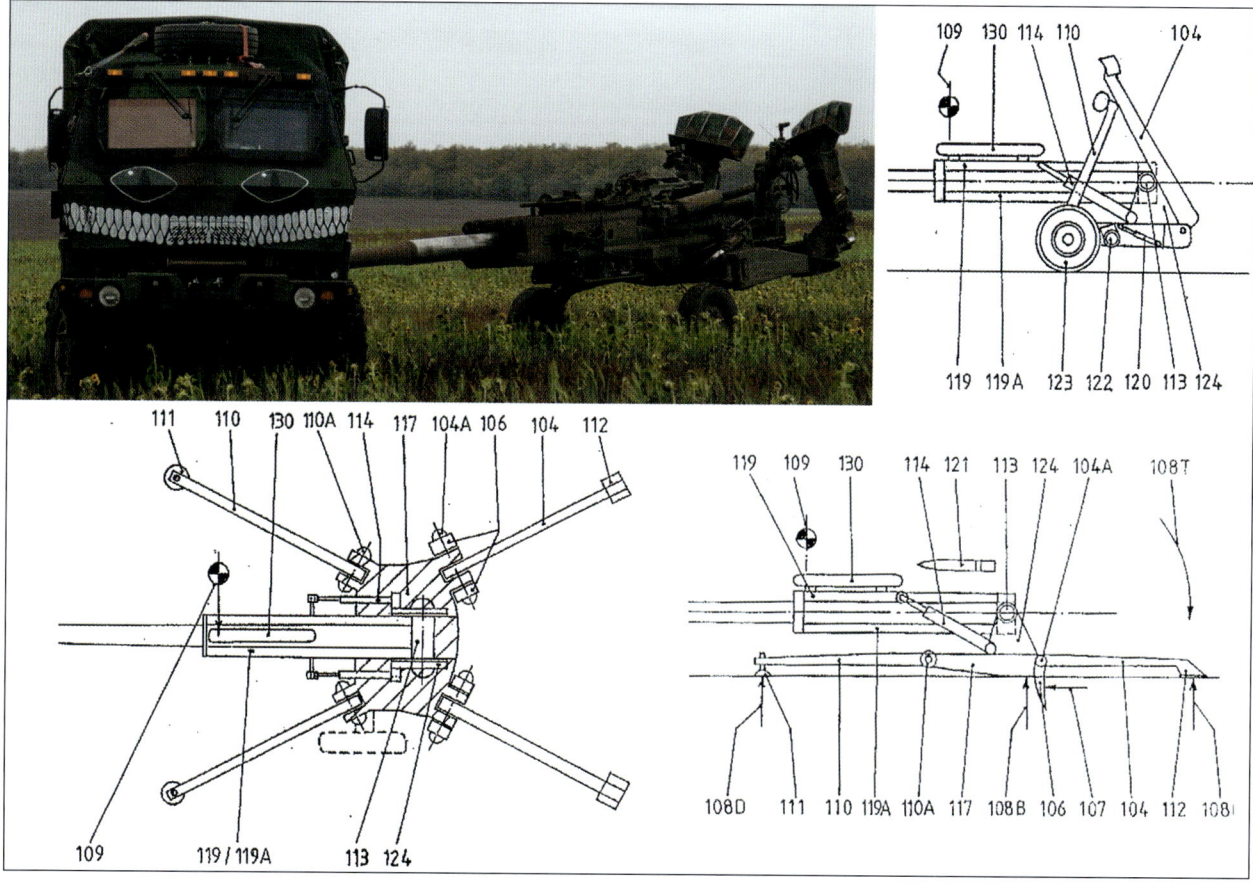

Ukrainian M777A2 of the 406th 'General Oleksa Almaziv' Artillery Brigade being towed by an Oshkosh M1083 6x6 MTV (Medium Tactical Vehicle) with LTAS (Long Term Armor Strategy) B-kit armoured cab and 'Cheshire Cat' face markings, Kherson front, October 2022. The black-and-white illustrations, taken from VSEL's patent filed in 1989 for a 'lightweight field howitzer', broadly describe the M777 in its traveling (a) and combat ((b), (c)) configurations. The most significant difference between the patent illustrations and production M777s are the front stabiliser legs (110), which fold sideways on M777s instead of upwards as in the illustrations. (ArmyInform; Deutsches Patentamt DE 39 43 508 A 1)

VSEL's UFH project manager Mike Macur once described its basic configuration as 'more like a recoiling mortar than a howitzer'. Indeed, the entire M777 carriage serves as a 'baseplate', transmitting the recoil energy not dissipated by the recoil system into the ground. It is deliberately designed to be front-heavy to counteract the overturning moment created by firing the gun. Four stabiliser legs provide a stable cruciform firing platform when deployed: the front legs are folded sideways and the rear legs with spades are folded upwards when not in use. Two wheels are fitted, mounted on Airlog hydrogas suspension units, allowing for a maximum towing speed of roads of 88km/h. The wheels also serve as hydraulic jacks: they are lowered using hand pumps to raise the howitzer for towing or for changing the firing direction (referred to as 'quickswitch' in the manufacturer's brochure). The basic structure of the M777 is mostly made of lightweight extruded titanium alloy. To keep costs down, only about 1t of titanium is used, and every titanium part has at least two functions: for example, the four titanium alloy tubes that provide structural rigidity for the gun cradle also act as pressure vessels for the pneumatic recoil system to vent nitrogen gas into. This combination of clever design and the use of titanium alloy allowed the production weight to be kept down to 3.8t (combat weight ~4.2t).[26]

Context

The first 'Triple Sevens', or '*Tri Sokiri*' ('Triple Axes' — '7' looks like an axe) to use the Ukrainian nickname, began arriving in Ukraine in April 2022. This was preceded by training of Ukrainian artillery personnel undertaken at NATO training grounds such as Grafenwoehr in Germany, where they received accelerated five-day courses on how to operate and maintain the system in the field.[27] At least 208 M777s have been delivered to Ukraine: the majority (198) are M777A2s from the US, with another six M777A2s from Australia and four M777C1s from Canada. This makes the M777 the most common Western artillery piece sent to Ukraine by a comfortable margin at the time of writing, and thus one of Ukraine's most important. Due to its L/39 barrel, the M777 is shorter ranged than L/52 systems and has to take up riskier positions closer to the frontline. Both of these facts are reflected by the fairly high number of losses suffered by the system: at least 54 destroyed, the most of any Ukrainian Western artillery system known at the time of writing.

The M777 does not have a real equivalent in the Russian military, as the towed 152mm howitzers like *Msta*-B are much heavier and not generally issued to the VDV for airborne operations. However, given the lack of such operations undertaken by either side since the early stages of the 2022 invasion, the M777 in Ukrainian service is exclusively used like an ordinary towed howitzer. As such, its light weight is less of an advantage, though it does allow lighter vehicles to be used: a civilian Ford Super Duty 4x4 pickup truck can tow the howitzer, as demonstrated on at least one occasion.[28] Some Ukrainian artillerymen have experience with both systems, such as 'Oleh' from 55 Art., who transitioned to the M777 from *Msta*-Bs in July 2022:

> Five days. We were trained by American experts. They actually didn't believe we'd do it. But we showed them what we can do on the *Mstas*. In terms of targeting, everything is the same, except for a couple of nuances. The *Msta* was large, fired short-range, and constantly leaked all over the place. This gun (M777) is more modern and reliable, it is more complicated, but we've gotten used to it.[29]

Ukrainian M777s without DFCS are mostly aimed like Soviet guns using the M137 panoramic telescope. While this is slower and more error-prone, it is a more rugged and reliable system, and one that most Ukrainian gunners would be used to. Later batches with DFCS should be a lot more capable and faster to get rounds off. On paper, the *Msta*-B and M777 are comparable in range (~24km), but there is a nuance. To achieve these ranges, the *Msta*-B must use the less-common extended-range hollow-base shells, while the M777 does this using the standard US M795 shell. When firing older 152mm ammunition, the *Msta*-B's range is limited to ~17km, while the M777 using the very common but older M107 round (used only for

Ukrainian M777 artilleryman prepares to use the EPIAFS on an M982A1 Excalibur PGM (centre). The handheld EPIAFS 'wand' is connected to a GPS control computer that sets the coordinates, and the wand is placed over the Excalibur's fuse to input the coordinates and fuse settings (right). The rocket-assisted Excalibur dramatically increases the range and accuracy of the M777, though it has proved highly susceptible to GPS jamming, to the point of being effectively useless according to some Ukrainian accounts. (ArmyInform)

One of 406 Art.'s M777s in action on the Kherson front, December 2022. In the earlier phases of the war, rapid displacement was the key to survival against Russian counterbattery fire. (ArmyInform)

training by the US) can still achieve 21km. The M777 also benefits from the US having developed modern long-range ammunition for it, such as the M549 RAP or Excalibur.

In light of the M777's well-received performance, its manufacturer BAE is restarting production to replace systems donated to Ukraine as well as in response to increased interest from potential customers. The last US Army order had been in 2019 and BAE had begun to shut down the production line as the last systems were delivered in February 2023.[30] The success of the M777 in Ukraine has also led to renewed focus on the viability of towed artillery on the modern high-intensity battlefield (see 'SP vs. Towed' box). Suffice to say, VSEL's private initiative from the 1980s has been a remarkably successful venture both in commercial (with well over 1,200 built) and military terms, and it will undoubtedly continue to be an important part of Ukraine's arsenal in its fight for survival against Russia. Asked which Western artillery system showed itself best in Ukraine, Colonel Musienko replied: '...the 155mm M777A2 proved to be the most effective and maintainable. Both by its characteristics and by the qualities that this gun possesses. And according to the conditions of use, it turned out to be the most suitable for modern warfare'.[31]

SP VS. TOWED: THE QUICK, THE CLEVER, AND THE DEAD

The Russo-Ukrainian War has rekindled debate on the viability of towed artillery systems in modern warfare. Both Russia and Ukraine are very heavily dependent on towed guns of various calibres, for there are not nearly enough SPGs available to completely replace them. However, Western militaries such as the US Army have apparently drawn the conclusion that towed artillery has no future in their arsenals. In fact, US Army Futures Command head General James Rainey went so far as to state his personal belief that '...we have witnessed the end of the effectiveness of towed artillery' in April 2024.[32] The US Army thus appears committed to phasing out its towed guns by 2030. But that begs the question: is this decision supported by combat experience in Ukraine?

SPGs have long enjoyed significant advantages over towed artillery in terms of their ability to react to calls for fire, conduct fire missions, and rapidly displace. As artillery fire control, reaction times, and counterbattery procedures improved throughout the Cold War, these attributes were seen as the best means for countering the primary perceived threat to artillery: counterbattery fire from the enemy's own artillery. This is best illustrated by the PzH 2000, which was designed to be able to fire 10 rounds and displace within two minutes while the expected time it would take Soviet artillery to react was thought to be about five minutes. Heavier tracked SPGs also tend to be better protected by armour against shell fragments as well as feature NBC protection, an important consideration for the Cold War where tactical nuclear and chemical weapons were expected to be used. In the early phases of the 2022 invasion, as well as during the Donbas War, the primary threat to Ukrainian artillery units was indeed counterbattery fire from opposing Russian artillery. While often crushing in fire superiority, Russian counterbattery also tended to be rather slow to react: by some accounts, usually taking 30 minutes to respond. Ukrainian towed and SP guns thus depended on rapid displacement in order to survive, and they were reportedly able to consistently evade Russian counterbattery fire during the first months of the invasion.[33]

However, since then, the battlefield has changed substantially. Frontlines have ossified as both sides have dug-in to entrenched positions behind minefields. UASs have also significantly proliferated, especially near lines of contact, resulting in a far more 'transparent' battlefield along with the ever-present threat of attack by loitering munitions such as the Russian *Lantset* or

Pions of 43 Art. firing at Russian targets in the Donbas, March 2022. At this early stage of the 2022 invasion, both sides often operated in the open, with the Ukrainians especially relying on rapid displacement to evade Russian counterbattery fire. (OTU *Skhid*)

FPVs with attached explosives. Under these circumstances, rapid displacement can be counterproductive since moving units are easier to spot, especially closer to the frontline where roads and other lines of supply are often placed under observation. Instead, both towed and SP guns operating close to the frontline have to rely on camouflage and entrenchment to survive under pervasive surveillance. In this respect, towed artillery pieces have significant advantages over SPGs due to their smaller size and logistical footprints, making them much easier to camouflage and entrench. This is especially true for light artillery such as the L119/M119 Light Gun and other 105mm pieces. Furthermore, the crew and ammunition for an emplaced towed gun can be dispersed, only coming together when the gun is ready to fire. This aids survivability in the event that the gun position is hit by counterbattery fire or loitering munitions, and is not really practical with an SPG. Furthermore, towed guns are generally significantly simpler and cheaper than SPGs; if the SPG has to be used from such static positions like a towed gun, the question naturally arises about whether the added cost is worth it?

Towed and SP artillery have their advantages and disadvantages. In the coming years, many nations will be evaluating their artillery arms, and thus these types of artillery within the context of the battles they expect to fight in the near future. While the SPG's speed in terms of mobility and reaction times can definitely be an asset in some situations, particularly when co-operating with and supporting mechanised forces in fast-moving offensives, the apparent superiority in survivability it was once thought to have had over towed artillery in the 1980s is not as clear on today's battlefield. It is the author's personal opinion that the Russo-Ukrainian War has shown that when skilfully employed, emplaced, and camouflaged, towed artillery can still be viable and survivable weapons in peer warfare, particularly as UASs proliferate around the world and the technology continues to evolve. As Colonel Musienko concluded: '… in no case can it be said that we need only towed or only SP guns. After all, we have different ways of using guns for different targets'.[34]

A well dug-in and camouflaged Russian D-30 somewhere in Ukraine in August 2024. The triangular lids can be closed to hide the howitzer from observation. (MORF)

3

M109: LONG-LIVED PALADIN

Development History

The origins of the remarkably evergreen M109 date back to a US Army meeting in 1952 on future requirements for SP artillery, which recommended SP mounts for the new 110mm T202 and 156mm T203 howitzers under development at the time: the T195 and T196. In 1956, the 110 and 156mm weapons were cancelled, as NATO had decided to standardise on the 105 and 155mm calibres, which led to the T195 and T196 being modified to take such weapons. Furthermore, the US Army now required both vehicles to share the same basic chassis design derived from the new M113 APC, necessitating a significant redesign. In these forms, the T195 and T196 were standardised as the 105mm Self-propelled Howitzer M108 and 155mm Self-propelled Howitzer M109, respectively, in 1963.[1] The M108 and M109 were intended to replace the 155mm M44 and 105mm M52 SPGs in American armoured and mechanised divisions. These had been developed hastily in response to a pressing need for more SP artillery due to the Korean War, and thus lacked some desired features that were incorporated into the new SPGs.[2]

Both the M108 and M109 first saw combat during the Vietnam War, but the M108 was fated to have a short career as it was, to put it bluntly, simply too much chassis for too little gun. The original M109 with its stubby M126 L/23 howitzer had been accepted into service on the condition that it could exceed the M44's 14.5km maximum range, for which the XM119 'super' charge had been developed. Unfortunately, it produced too much muzzle blast, with detrimental effects on the crew and vehicle components alike. Thus, the M126 was restricted to the same short range. This led to the introduction of the longer 155mm M185 L/39 howitzer on the M109A1 (conversion of existing M109s) and M109A1B (new-build) models in the early 1970s. Further improvements, such as a ballistic

M109A6 Paladin of the 47th 'Magura' Mechanised Brigade, July 2023. The background has been censored to prevent geolocation. The Paladin is most easily recognised by the ballistic shield on its gun mechanisms, the remote-controlled travel lock for the gun barrel, and the more angular turret. (47 Mech.)

Belgian M108 (left) and Dutch M109 (right). The M108 and M109 are virtually identical externally save for the gun. The original M109 is seen here with the stubby 155mm M126 L/23 howitzer. (Jean-Pol Grandmont; R. Kersten (Leger Film- en Fotodienst)

M109A3GN in service with the 72nd 'Black Zaporizhzhians' Mechanised Brigade, Donetsk front, January 2023. Note the armoured cover for the panoramic telescope, introduced on M109A2/A3s. (ZSU)

cover for the gunner's panoramic telescope, increased ammunition capacity with an extended turret bustle, and improved gun recoil system and rammer led to the introduction of the M109A2 in 1976. Existing M109A1/A1Bs were also converted to the new standard as M109A3/A3Bs.[3]

In the early 1980s, in order to cut costs, the US Army instituted the Howitzer Extended Life Program (HELP) for the M109 instead of ordering a new system. This mostly concentrated on fixing the deficiencies and reliability issues suffered by the earlier models, as well as improving the NBC protection, resulting in the M109A4 standard to which existing M109A2/A3s were converted. However, this was also immediately recognised as insufficient, and the following 1985 Howitzer Improvement Program (HIP) would introduce the most significant upgrade to the M109's capabilities. As noted in the Soviet-legacy guns volume, the 1970s and 1980s marked a period of rapid modernisation for the Soviet artillery both qualitatively and quantitatively (ironically, some of it driven by the M109's introduction). Thus, the HIP envisioned rapid emplacement, firing, and displacement capabilities to increase both the howitzer's survivability and ability to mass fires. To achieve this required a near complete modernisation of the M109: many options were tested, but the final product had the new 155mm M284 L/39 howitzer, an automated FCS, improved suspension, a new turret with increased ammunition capacity, and microclimate cooling for the crew. This was standardised as the M109A6 and nicknamed 'Paladin'. The first Paladins were delivered to the US Army in 1992. At the time, the US Army had over 2,400 M109s in its inventory, and a more economical upgrade with some of the Paladin's features (most notably the M284 howitzer) was developed for them, designated M109A5.[4]

In addition to US service, the M109 would go on to become the 'standard' SPG for NATO forces and other US allies, with a bewildering number of variants developed and licence production undertaken by a number of nations such as the FRG (Federal Republic of Germany), Italy, and the ROK. It is not possible to cover all of these variants in detail within the limits of this book. Variants known to be used by Ukraine at the time of writing are as follows:

- M109A3GN: German-produced M109Gs upgraded to the M109A3 standard with Rheinmetall L/39 barrel sold to Norway. Retired from Norwegian service in 2020 and replaced by K9 VIDAR. At least 23 provided by Norway to Ukraine.

- M109A4 BE: Belgian M109A2/A3 upgraded under 2008 MLU (Mid-Life Update) M109 programme. Includes semi-automatic loader, 1.2kW diesel APU, Dutch RDM Improved Ballistic Turret, and improved hydraulic traverse. Retired almost immediately after upgrade when the Belgian Army abandoned tracked vehicles (so much for a 'mid-life' update…). Sold to private companies, from which 28 were bought by the UK and donated to Ukraine.[5]
- M109L: original M109s bought by Italy without armament and fitted with an OTO Melara[6] 155mm L/39 howitzer ballistically identical to the towed FH70 howitzer. Hull modified to M109A3 standard. Retired in the 2000s from Italian service and replaced by PzH 2000. At least 60 sent to Ukraine by Italy.
- M109A5Ö: M109A2/A3/A5s bought by Austria ('Ö' — Österreich) and modernised with Austrian components such as the NORA (*Navigations-, Orientierungs- und Richtanlage*, Navigation, Orientation, and Pointing System) INS, EAFLS (*Elektronische Artillerie Feuerleitsystem*, Electronic Artillery FCS) automated FCS, and Intertechnik Linz semi-automatic loader. Retired from Austrian service in 2010, 53 sold to Latvia, of which at least six have been sent to Ukraine.[7]
- M109A6 Paladin: at least 18 sent by the US in January 2023. This is the most modern variant used by Ukraine.

Strictly speaking, the name 'Paladin' only applies to the M109A6 and the latest US model, the M109A7 (which was at one point known as the M109A6 Paladin Integrated Management (PIM)). It is not uncommon to see the name applied to other M109 models; however, in this text, 'Paladin' refers strictly to the M109A6. Regrettably, the author does not have access to much documentation about the M109L or M109A5Ö, thus the following technical summary will focus on the M109A3GN/A4 BE and M109A6 Paladin. However, they are from the same generations, respectively, and thus roughly comparable in capability.

Technical Summary

All M109 variants in Ukrainian service use a 155mm L/39 howitzer as their primary armament. However, the ordnances are not identical to each other: the M109A4 BE has the standard 155mm M185 on M178 mount, the M109A3GN has a Rheinmetall ordnance, the M109L has an OTO Melara 155mm ordnance, and the M109A5Ö and Paladin use the 155mm M284 on M182A1 mounting. With the standard US 46.9kg M795 projectile and extended-range M203A1 (Zone 8) charge propelling it at 802m/s (or European equivalent ammunition), the latter four can reach up to 24km range; 30km with M549A1 RAP. The older M185 is not rated to use M203A1 charges and is restricted to weaker charges like M119A1, which limits its range to 23.5km even with RAP.[8] All except the M109A3GN use a semi-automatic interrupted screw breech mechanism; the M109A3GN has a horizontal sliding-block breech with an obturator. While the original M109 was manually loaded, most models developed since feature a hydraulic loader-rammer to assist the loaders in pushing the heavy projectiles into the breech. However, the M109A4 BE and M109A5Ö have more modern semi-automatic loaders with flick rammers for their projectiles. In all cases, the charges are loaded manually. The Paladin's technical manual gives a maximum rate-of-fire of four rounds/minute for three minutes and a sustained rate-of-fire of one round/minute. The M109A5 BE and M109A5Ö's semi-automatic loaders allow for burst fire capability (three rounds in 20 seconds, six rounds in one minute for the former; three rounds in 15 seconds, 10 rounds in one minute for the latter).[9, 10]

All variants of the M109 can elevate the gun up to 75°, allowing for high-arcing trajectories and a lower minimum range for indirect fire. They also have full 360° traverse thanks to the turret. In older models such as the M109A3GN, M109A4 BE, and M109L, aiming is done the old-fashioned way using a panoramic telescope for indirect fire (the model used can vary depending on the nation of origin).[11] There is also the M118 elbow telescope with M42 periscope for direct fire. These systems remain as back-ups for the M109A5Ö and Paladin's more advanced systems. The Paladin has the appropriately named Paladin Digital Fire Control System (PDFCS): it receives target information, calculates weapons position, and automatically lays the gun. It can do this using coordinates received directly from

M109L of the 37th Marine Brigade on the Zaporizhzhia front, July 2023. The M109L can be recognised by its Italian-made muzzle brake taken from the FH70 towed howitzer (inset). (United24)

the unit requesting fire support or forward observers, if necessary. In its full form, it also includes the Defense Advanced GPS Receiver (DAGR) for navigation, Platform Integration Kit (PIK), and EPIAFS for compatibility with the Excalibur PGM. It is not publicly known at the time of writing whether Ukraine has received the full PDFCS or whether elements of it have been stripped out as with the DFCS on M119A3s and M777A2s (see L119 & M777). The M109A5Ö's NORA and EAFLS systems perform most of the same fire control and navigation functions as PDFCS, although it is unknown if it has the EPIAFS or similar system needed to fire Excalibur.[12] With the full PDFCS, a Paladin can open fire within 30 seconds of occupying a firing position, while an older M109 would be significantly slower: the Germans rated the M109A3G as taking two and a half minutes to do the same.[13, 14]

One of 47 Mech.'s Paladins firing at Russian targets on the Pokrovsk front, July 2024. The Paladin has a noticeably longer turret bustle than earlier M109 models to fit more ammunition. (47 Mech.)

Top: using the hydraulic loader-rammer in a Paladin. Rounds are placed on the loading tray and pushed into the breech by hand before the rammer is moved into position and the round is rammed further into the breech. The rammer and tray are both stowed away before the gun is fired. Bottom: the semi-automatic loader with flick rammer of the M109A5Ö. The second loader is holding M231 modular charges. A similar design was offered for the Paladin, but the US Army cheaped out and kept the old hydraulic rammer. Western 155mm guns use bagged/modular charges, thus a primer has to be inserted in the breech before firing. This is done manually in most M109s (the M109A3GN and A5Ö have primer magazine feeds: for whatever reason, the loader in this A5Ö is loading the primer cartridge manually), as seen in the bottom right. (ZSU StratCom; 92 Assault)

US Army Paladins are equipped with the AN/VIC-3(V)-6 intercom and AN/VRC-89A radio set, which is a part of the Single Channel Ground and Airborne Radio System (SINCGARS) combat radio network used by the US and allied militaries. It is unknown if this radio is used on Ukrainian Paladins. The M109A5Ö has the older AN/VRC-64A-0 radio set and AN/VIC-1 intercom. Older M109A1/A2/A3/A4s did not originally have radio sets and only had the AN/VIC-1 intercom, though some in US Army service were later fitted with AN/VRC-89 or other SINCGARS radios: it is unknown what is used on Ukrainian M109A3GNs, M109Ls, or M109A4 BEs.[15]

Ammunition stowage differs based on the model. The Paladin can carry up to 39 projectiles and 44 charges. All charges are stored exclusively in the turret bustle, which also has a ready rack for six projectiles. The remaining projectiles are stored in the hull. Older models are limited to 36 projectiles (22 turret, 14 hull) and charges (14 turret, 22 hull) each. All M109 models feature doors in the turret bustle and hull rear to allow ammunition to be resupplied externally. The US Army has a dedicated ammunition resupply vehicle for its M109A6/A7 Paladins, the M992 Field Artillery Ammunition Support Vehicle (FAASV), which can carry up to 95 complete rounds. However, only 30 of these are known to have been provided to Ukraine: insufficient to support all of their M109s.

As is tradition for American armoured fighting vehicles (AFVs), all M109 variants are also armed with a .50 (12.7mm) Browning M2 heavy MG with 500 rounds for defence against low-flying aircraft and soft ground targets. The Paladin even has racks for three M136 AT4 single-shot recoilless anti-tank weapons, though these are unlikely to be used except in the direst of circumstances. To keep its weight down, M109s are made of rolled 5083 aluminium alloy plates up to 32mm thick. On the Paladin, this protection is augmented by steel applique armour on the turret bustle sides and aramid spall liners. Pre-Paladin M109s have a crew of six: driver, commander, gunner, assistant gunner, and two loaders. The gunner would set the gun direction, while the assistant gunner was responsible for setting elevation (although one-man laying was possible). One loader would actually load and operate the gun, while the other would set fuses. From the M109A6 onwards, the crew was reduced to four, the assistant gunner and second loader being dispensed with.[16] The M109A3GN and M109A5Ö also feature six smoke grenade launchers mounted on the turret.

All variants of the M109 up to the M109A6 are powered by the 411hp 8V71T two-stroke turbocharged V-8 diesel engine. The

The old and the new: panoramic telescope in M109A3GN (left, note the horizontal sliding-block breech), PDFCS display unit in Paladin (middle), and NORA display unit in M109A5Ö (right). (ArmyInform; ArmyTV; O!Nebylovych)

Left: restocking the turret bustle projectile racks on a Ukrainian Marines M109L. In Paladins, the turret bustle stores all the charges instead, with only six projectiles within a ready rack. Right: .50 M2 heavy MG on the commander's cupola of a Paladin. This is normally removed by the Ukrainians. (United24; 47 Mech.)

earlier M109s weigh approximately 25t combat loaded, while the M109A6 is considerably heavier at 28.9t. These give power/weight ratios of 16.4hp/t and 14.2hp/t, respectively. The transmission used on earlier M109s is the Allison XTG-411-2A, while the M109A6 uses the improved XTG-411-4. Both have four forward and two reverse gears, allowing for a top road speed of 56km/h and 61km/h, respectively, and a maximum reverse speed of 11km/h. The torsion bar suspension, derived from the M113, consists of seven road wheels on each side, with high capacity hydraulic shock absorbers on the first and last wheels; Paladins have improved high strength torsion bars. Dual-pin steel tracks with removable rubber pads are used on all M109s. All M109s also have two manually operated spades on each side of the rear hull door.[17] The manuals recommend using them when firing off of loose, sandy, or muddy soils and also state that they must be used when firing while the M109 is mated to an M992 FAASV.[18, 19] However, the Ukrainians do not seem to use the spades at all even in muddy terrain, and doing the latter almost never happens in Ukraine as it is highly dangerous on a transparent battlefield filled with UASs.

Context

With over 50 years of service behind it from the jungles of South East Asia to the deserts of the Middle East, the venerable M109 once again finds itself in combat, this time in Europe: the battlefield it was originally envisaged for. Norway was the first to announce sending its M109A3GNs in April 2022, to be followed by the UK, Italy, Latvia, and the US. Over 120 M109s of all models have been sent, making it the most numerous SPG donated to Ukraine at the time of writing. Most of these seem to have been delivered to tank, mechanised, and assault brigades, where they would presumably replace or supplement the *Akatsiya*.

In terms of capabilities, the M109s used in Ukraine can be roughly divided into two categories. The second generation ones (M109A3GN, M109L, and M109A4 BE) are roughly equivalent to the *Akatsiya* in terms of fire control, reaction time, and most other combat characteristics, though the M109L can achieve substantially better ranges with its FH70-derived ordnance. As many Ukrainian artillerymen trained on older systems like the *Akatsiya*, they usually have not had many problems transferring to these models, and they

Left: 8V71T engine, part of the very successful Series 71 engines from Detroit Diesel, a subsidiary of General Motors. It also powered the M107, M108, and M110. Right: M109A5Ö of the 92nd 'Ivan Sirko' Mechanised Brigade undergoing maintenance with the engine deck open. (Thomas Vogt; O!Nebylovych)

M109A5Ö of the 92nd 'Ivan Sirko' Mechanised Brigade on the Bakhmut front, November 2023. The M109A5Ö has distinctive rear turret stowage boxes. (O!Nebylovych)

Left: Ex-US Army Paladin being shipped to Ukraine near Ferch, Germany, March 2023. Right: M109A4 BE 'Svotyk' in service with the 17th 'Kostiantyn Pestushko' Tank Brigade, January 2023. Few SPGs have demonstrated such growth potential over their careers as the M109. (Georgfoto (Wikimedia); 17 Tank)

seem to be well-liked. 'Andriy' of the 17th 'Kostiantyn Pestushko' Tank Brigade had this to say about his M109A4 BE: 'The principle is the same in all SPGs, but compared to ours [ex-Soviet ones], the calibre here is larger, and they are more accurate and carry more shells. In general, the machine shows itself well, we are satisfied with it'.[20]

The third generation, represented by the Paladin and M109A5Ö, are substantially more advanced than the *Akatsiya* and basic *Msta*-S, and are more comparable to the most advanced Russian SPG in large-scale service, *Msta*-SM2, in range and fire control. Relatively few of these have been sent, and they seem to have been reserved for the new Western-equipped 47th 'Mahura' Mechanised Brigade and a few elite units such as the 92nd 'Ivan Sirko' Assault and 93rd 'Kholodnyi Yar' Mechanised Brigades. Users from these units have praised the advanced FCSs, which provide capabilities previously impossible with the Soviet-legacy artillery pieces. 'Garik', a mechanic from 92 Mech., compared the M109A5Ö to the *Akatsiya*: 'Aiming here is generally perfect because here everything goes through the computer…there are crews that bask in it [M109], saying "We don't want to go back [to the Akatsiya]. Leave her [M109] in drivable condition and we will work with pleasure"'.[21] He also compared the M109 favourably to the *Akatsiya* in terms of maintenance, saying it was easier to access and replace parts.

M109s also generally have a significantly shorter range than newer 155mm SPGs equipped with L/52 barrels, which means they must operate closer to the frontlines like the M777. This, as well as the large number of M109s in Ukrainian service, is reflected in the number destroyed (49), the highest among Western SPGs and second only to the *Gvozdika* among all SPGs in Ukrainian service. However, there are far more M109s around than any other Western systems because the M109 was used by nearly all NATO nations at some point and remains in widespread service with the US Army and other militaries around the world. There are possibly still significant numbers of M109s available in storage that could be sent immediately or after refurbishment if needed, and it is thus not out of the question that more will be sent to Ukraine in the future.

The venerable M109 has proved itself time and again to be one of the most successful SPG designs of the Cold War. Since the 1970s, the US Army has attempted to find a replacement for the M109, but all of these programmes have never come to fruition for one reason or another. Most recently, the XM1203 Non-Line-of-Sight Cannon (NLOS-C) was cancelled in 2009, leading to the development of the M109A7 instead. It is thus the M109 that will form the backbone of the US Army's SPG fleet for the foreseeable future. Its performance in Ukraine may indicate that its time is not up yet.

INTERVIEW WITH A UKRAINIAN PALADIN GUNNER

The following is an interview the author (A) conducted with an M109A6 Paladin gunner (P) of the 47th Mechanised Brigade, who goes by the Twitter handle of @prekrasnii1, in November 2024 and published with his kind permission. The author has reformatted the DMs into a more easily readable format, but has otherwise attempted to preserve as much as possible.

A: In your experience, how reliable is the Paladin? PzH 2000 and *Zuzana* have gained a bit of a bad reputation but I'm curious if you have encountered similar problems with the Paladin?

P: I would describe Paladin as a very reliable system. The artillery part almost never failed us, and I guess a few problems that we had were related to extensive use and a lack of expertise for our technicians and spare parts. Every barrel was new when we received it and also we had an opportunity to replace one as it was worn (some higher level technicians check it with a borescope regularly).

But usually we do have problems with the chassis. Our first problem was that we received vehicles in bad condition. Only one SPG out of four didn't have major problems. As it was shipped, one required tracks replacement (it was replaced with M109A3 tracks), another required engine replacement after we checked oil and found "*struzhka*" (*author: metal shavings*) there (it was replaced with an M109L's engine), the other had a broken generator and electrical system problems.

Two M109A6 Paladins of 47 Mech. The front Paladin has broken down and its ammunition is being transferred to the other Paladin before being taken away for repairs. (@prekrasnii1)

    Actually, the generators are unreliable: even when there were no mistakes from our side, they just break from time to time. But our repairs were also low quality, sometimes to the point that after they replaced transmission they forgot to screw it properly, so it lost all the oil on the way to operations area, and many more such cases. One of our vehicles is under repair in Poland for almost a year now but we cannibalised almost everything from it for other guns. Also, I should say that our training guns in Germany were not in great condition.

    On the problems with the shipped condition: my SPG didn't even have screws on the muzzle brake and bore evacuator, so we asked a master to recreate it, as we had samples from the others. There was also a problem with the BII (basic issues items): it was incomplete and something necessary that we couldn't find in Ukraine.

A: Does your Paladin have the full fire control system? Earlier in the war, the US stripped the DFCS from M777s and M119s before sending it to Ukraine, and the Paladin's DFCS is similar in principle.

P: Yes, we have full PDFCS and it is the best. Very accurate and allow us to have more creative firing positions since we do not require 'reference points' (I don't remember the English term). We almost never use the panoramic telescope. We had a special software version for Ukraine (in English), but I didn't notice any major difference with what we had on the training in Germany.

    As far as I remember we didn't receive DAGRs (*author: AN/PSN-13 Defense Advanced GPS Receiver*) initially. But during the Kursk offensive we already had them. Anyway, they were crucial only for Excalibur rounds, which are rare and effectively countered by the Russians.

A: Do you have experience with other systems or only the Paladin? If you have with others, how do they compare in your opinion?

P: I don't have experience with other systems. When we show the insides for other guys from Soviet systems (artillery/tanks), their first reaction is: 'Wow! There is so much free space for a crew'. The whole crew can sleep inside.

A: Do you find the shorter range problematic, since the Paladin has a shorter range than systems like *Krab* or PzH 2000 using standard ammo?

P: Not usually problematic. Our job is the frontlines mostly and I find smaller charges are more accurate (M231 and M3A1 ❤). During the battle for Avdiivka, we were 2–5km from the front lines. On the Kursk front, it's harder because we are surrounded and the terrain is mostly open fields. Also, right now we have a fire point 200 m from the *Krabs* 😄. The drawback is that we aren't always able to reach the enemy artillery.

A: Is Russian counterbattery much of an issue or is the problem more drones?

P: Usually it's 1–4 random rounds from the Russians once/twice a day within 300 m. When we recognize corrected fire for elimination then we usually change position. Drones are scarier but we don't move much. Our battery is lucky not to lose a single person/vehicle to either. But on the artillery division level it is a different story.

A: I'm assuming your unit has received the FAAASV along with Paladin. Is it used for resupply or is it too big a target?

P: Yes, we received them. Our battery does not use it for resupply because of the reason you stated. Other batteries did but lately it was decided not to because of the case with a destroyed SPG.

    I guess it is better to use wheeled vehicles for resupply and leave less tracks to the firing position.

A: Do they have any particular use then?

P: Stationary storage. During the offensive, we had a lot of ammo so we kept them close.

A: What do you think is the biggest difference between the training you received from the US and the reality of artillery fighting in Ukraine?

P: Maintenance. If you have access to the operator's manual you'll see that there is only basic troubleshooting and absence of information about the system. We very often had an answer from American operators: 'Our technicians do this. We don't know'. In Ukraine, we can't allow this due to lack of infrastructure and that we are forced to do maintenance and light repairs in the firing position.

    Also, shoot and scoot isn't great idea in our reality. At least for tracked L/39 systems.

A: Is there any advantage then to having a fast reaction speed or advanced FCS?

P: Yes. We don't need a gunner and we can hide the SPG deeper because we aren't bound to reference points and can move the gun out of the hideout without losing our orientation. Without the gunner, we eliminate human error and can lay the gun faster.

A: The Paladin comes with a .50 MG, does it have any use (e.g. against drones)?

P: No. Useless. And we would often get them caught on some positions since they are placed higher than the hatch. We gave them to the infantry.

A: Do you often have to respond to calls for fire from different directions? Part of the logic behind having the turret in the design was for this reason.

P: Yes. During the chaotic "counteroffensive" [author: 2023 Zaporizhzhia counteroffensive]. Later not so often.

A: You said Excalibur has been completely countered by the Russians, does that mean it is no longer used at all?

P: At least we do not use it at all.

A: I saw that the US has provided Copperhead as well, but it seems like the utility might also be limited since it needs a laser designator. Have you any experience with it?

P: I can't say.

A: If you could make any improvements to the Paladin, what would you do?

P: Faster PDFCS loading (now it takes ~7 min, so we are forced to leave it working all the time).

As far as I know the M109A7 moved from hydraulic to electrical traverse. It may be a great improvement but I don't have experience.

More unified storage for propellants. For example M119 doesn't fit in regular slots. We don't unpack any canisters before loading because of safety and humidity. And we store massive canisters on the floor under the breech.

In order to check the engine and fix some disconnected tubes or whatever trivial problem, we must lift the whole engine with a crane. So more access to the powerpack would be nice.

The hydraulic loader is badly designed. Almost no difference with manual loading and it eats up space.

4
PANZERHAUBITZE 2000: THE GOLD STANDARD

Development History

Throughout the 1950s and 1960s, the newly-reformed Italian and (West) German armies were almost completely dependent on American military equipment, as their own military industries had been obliterated by the Allied forces during the Second World War. Artillery was no exception, and the *Esercito Italiano* and *Bundeswehr* were equipped with American-designed towed and SP artillery such as the M109, with local modifications. The UK had also bought the M109 as an interim measure while it phased out its non-NATO standard calibre weapons such as the BL 5.5-inch (140mm) Medium Gun in favour of 155mm weapons. Lacking the Americans' resources or industrial base but also wanting to avoid being purely reliant on the US, the European nations have often turned to joint multinational projects in order to pool their resources and efforts. These efforts have sometimes eventually been successful, as was the case with the Panavia Tornado MRCA or Eurofighter Typhoon. However, they have also often failed due to irreconcilable requirements from the different militaries or political differences (e.g. the German-American MBT70 project).

In the 1970s, the UK, Germany, and Italy agreed to jointly develop 155mm towed and SP artillery pieces in parallel to replace their existing 155mm weapons. Their requirements included: a high rate-of-fire with burst capability, high mobility with minimal emplacement time, and a long range. These projects were known in English as FH70 ('Field Howitzer of the 1970s') and SP70 ('Self-Propelled Gun of the 1970s'), respectively. The former's development was led by the UK, while the latter was led by Germany (also called 'PzH (*Panzerhaubitze*, lit. armoured howitzer) 155-1'. The FH70's development proceeded relatively well, with the first series examples delivered in 1978. The FH70 (or 'FH 155-1' in German) has proven to be rather successful in European service and on the export market; some of them are currently in action in Ukraine.

On the other hand, the SP70 suffered from a very protracted and troubled development. Numerous technical problems and some poor design choices led to continual delays and cost overruns, so that the first prototypes built from armour plate were not ready until 1984. By that time, the writing was clearly on the wall and all three nations pulled out from the SP70 project in 1986, opting to go their separate ways in developing their next-generation SPGs.[1] The British would eventually develop the AS90, to be described later, while Italy opted to instead buy M109s from the US without armament and fit them with an FH70-derived weapon as the M109L, described previously in the M109 section.

That left Germany to also develop its own successor for the M109. In fact, as early as fall 1986, the PzH 155-FT (Fronttrieb, Front drive) project was initiated. The initial requirements were highly ambitious: an unassisted range of 30km with L15 shells; automated gun-laying; ammunition capacity of 48 rounds or, preferably, 60 rounds; turret mass not exceeding 16t. These would later be expanded to include the ability to open fire within 30 seconds of receiving an order while on the march, fire eight rounds in one minute, and displace in another 30 seconds. At the time, there were six German firms involved in AFV production, five of whom consolidated in 1987 into two consortia by geographical location to pitch their designs for the PzH 155-FT: North (Wegmann, MaK) and South (Krauss-Maffei, Rheinmetall, KuKa). A demonstrator prototype from each consortium was completed in 1990 and underwent testing as part of the first project stage.[2] That same year the North consortium's design was chosen for what was now called 'PzH 2000', with Wegmann as the primary contractor. Four more prototypes were completed and tested from 1990 to 1995, and upon their successful completion the PzH 2000 was accepted into service by the *Bundeswehr* at the end of 1995.[3]

The *Bundeswehr* would purchase 185 PzH 2000s, delivered 1998–2002. These were modernised to the A1 standard, primarily

PzH 2000 of the 43rd 'Taras Triasylo' Artillery Brigade, January 2025. An exceptionally capable system, the PzH 2000 is well-liked by Ukrainian crews, but its advanced features come at significant costs, both financial and logistical. (43 Art.)

FH70 in service with the 44th 'Hetman Danylo Apostol' Artillery Brigade, November 2022. At least 34 have been donated by Italy and Estonia to Ukraine, where they are described as 'incredibly accurate and easy to use'. At the bottom, it is seen being towed by Italian-donated Astra ACTL SM 66.40 CAD 6x6 trucks, but like many late Cold War Western towed artillery designs, the FH70 has an APU to power its hydraulic mechanisms and provide limited SP movement on the battlefield. (MOU)

PzH 155-1 (SP70) prototype scale model in the *Wehrtechnische Sammlung der Bundeswehr*. The PzH 155-1 was based on the Leopard 1 chassis and the resulting turret placement necessitated an external conveyor for feeding ammunition into the turret to the gun (similar to the Soviet *Msta*-S). This awkward arrangement proved to be unreliable and fragile, one of many, many problems that ultimately killed the project. (Clemens Vasters; Deutsches Patentamt DE 3627262)

integrating software upgrades (among other things, moving the MICMOS fire control computer from Windows 3.11 to Windows 2000) and improvements to the loading system. Thirty-four were modified to the A2 standard with improved cooling for the combat compartment and propellant charges for service in Afghanistan. The Italians, who had decided not to develop their own system following the cancellation of SP70 and waited instead to see how the British and Germans got on with their developments, eventually chose the PzH 2000 and negotiated a workshare agreement where 50 percent of the parts would be made by an Italian consortium of Fiat/Iveco and OTO Melara. They manufactured 68 PzH 2000ITs from 2005 to 2010, with minor modifications to suit Italian requirements. The Dutch also bought 57 PzH 2000s to replace its M109s in 2001. These also had some minor modifications to suit Dutch specifications as PzH 2000NLs.[4] Ukraine has received PzH 2000s from all three nations; however, in the technical summary, only the German PzH 2000 A1 will be described in detail, as for most practical purposes these systems do not differ significantly in capability.

Technical Summary

To meet the required 30km range with unassisted projectiles, the PzH 2000 A1 uses a JBMoU-compliant 155mm L/52 Rheinmetall ordnance. It was the first SPG to enter service with such a weapon, setting the standard for modern post-Cold War 155mm SPGs. The barrel bore is chrome-plated and laser-hardened to increase durability and barrel life. The breech is of the vertical sliding-block

PzH 2000 of 43 Art. firing at Russian targets. Modern 155mm systems are, on paper, comparable in firepower to older 203mm systems thanks to their significantly higher rate-of-fire. (Arsenii Gerasymenko)

(A) The PzH 2000's *Geschosstransporter* (GS), used to (B) transfer rounds between the *Transportschiene* (TS) and the magazine racks, which are arranged radially from the middle of the vehicle. It has a seat, allowing the loader to control it manually if needed. The TS is a rotating platform with a flip-up tray that transfers projectiles inserted horizontally from the hull rear (C) to the GS (D) or from the GS to the *Geschoss-Übergabearm* (GÜBA). The GÜBA (E) raises the projectile to the loading line and its flick rammer accelerates the projectile (F, G) into the breech (H). Here it is seen with DM121 extended-range HE. In (F), the Ukrainian loader is placing the projectile on the GÜBA manually, effectively relegating it to being a semi-automatic loader-rammer. (ArmyTV, United24)

breech type with an obturator. Projectiles are fed by a relatively complex and unique autoloading system known in German as the *Munitionsfluss* ('ammunition flow'). It consists of several components: hull projectile magazine, *Geschosstransporter* (GS), *Transportschiene* (TS), *Geschoss-Übergabearm* (GÜBA), and their associated control systems.[5] These allow the projectile loading process (including fuse-setting and restocking the projectile magazine) to be fully automated (charges are still loaded manually by a loader). The GÜBA is fitted with a pneumatic flick rammer, the first to be fitted on any SPG, allowing for a much higher rate-of-fire than previous hydraulic or chain rammer systems. The PzH 2000 has demonstrated three rounds fired in 9.2 seconds, 10 rounds in 56.2 seconds, and 20 rounds in two minutes 10 seconds during testing: an impressive achievement by any standard.[6] Restocking of the complete ammunition load (60 projectiles + up to 288 modular charges) can be done in under 11 minutes.

Fire control is autonomous using the onboard MICMOS 2000 ballistics computer, muzzle velocity management and measurement system, and hybrid INS/SNS. The PzH 2000's fire control computer was also the first to be integrated with the NATO Armament Ballistic Kernel (NABK), a software package that takes in fire control inputs such as projectile and charge properties and meteorological conditions to compute trajectories and fire solutions. This allows it to be quickly modified to integrate nation-specific 155mm ammunition.[7] The PzH 2000 can receive target engagement data via the FüWES (*Führungs- und Waffeneinsatzsystem*, Command and weapon deployment system) ADLER (*Artillerie-, Daten-, Lage- und Einsatz-Rechnerverbund*, Artillery, data, situation, and deployment computer network) BMS's (battlefield management system) datalink, be ready to open fire within 30 seconds of stopping, fire 10 rounds in one minute, and be ready to displace within 30 seconds.[8] The vehicle is naturally equipped with a modern digital radio and intercom, though the exact models have not been publicly disclosed.

PzH 2000 is also MRSI-capable: firing five rounds in sequentially lower trajectories so that all five shells impact the target simultaneously.[9] Under normal circumstances, due to the high

Top: 'Oleksii' of 43 Art. demonstrates the charge storage on the PzH 2000 under his command. When not in use, the charges are sealed off behind a door. His BASys control terminal can be seen to the left, with the PERI RTNL80 above. Bottom: a close-up view of the *Igelplatten* on the turret roof of a PzH 2000. The PERI RTNL80 sight is seen protruding above. (ArmyTV, United24; 43 Art.)

level of automation, the commander is the gunner responsible for selecting targets and firing the gun, with the designated 'gunner' acting as an assistant gunner and loader, only taking over under certain conditions such as if the MICMOS fails. In such a situation, the gunner can mount the PERI R19 panoramic sight to conduct indirect fire. The gunner also has a PzF TN 80 direct-fire telescope for the unlikely event that the PzH 2000 should find itself in direct-fire engagements, while the commander has the PERI RTNL80 panoramic sight. The gun can be elevated up to 65° and the turret has unlimited 360° traverse, allowing the PzH 2000 to quickly respond to calls for fire in any direction.

Much attention has been paid to survivability in the PzH 2000, arguably more than in any other indirect fire SPG to date. The basic steel RHA protection is rated against 14.5mm armour piercing bullets and shrapnel from Soviet 152mm HE-Fragmentation shells. This protection is augmented by spall liners, as well as applique protection sometimes known as *Igelpanzerung* (lit. 'hedgehog armour') on the turret roof and driver's compartment. It consists of panels of 60mm rubber spikes (*Igelplatten*) that dissipate the explosive energy or shaped charges of bomblets from cluster munitions.[10] Propellant charges, which are more likely than shells to detonate or deflagrate when hit, are stored exclusively in isolated compartments in the turret rear. A decision was also made not to use hydraulic mechanisms in the PzH 2000's crew compartment due to the potentially flammable hydraulic fluid: the gun-laying and turret traverse drives and *Munitionsfluss* components are all electrically powered. Fire suppression systems are also fitted for both the engine and crew compartments, along with NBC protection. The PzH 2000 has a crew of five: driver, gunner, commander, and two loaders. One of the loaders also has a 7.62-mm MG3 anti-aircraft machine gun (AAMG) on their hatch for close-in protection; the amount of ammunition carried has not been disclosed.[11] In addition, eight smoke grenade launchers are provided, four mounted on each side of the gun.

At 55t (56–57t for the A2), the PzH 2000 is the heaviest SPG currently in service, weighing more than even the mighty Soviet-legacy *Pion*. It is powered by the 1,000hp MTU-88 1 turbocharged 4-stroke V-8 diesel engine with intercooling, derived from the Leopard 1 MBT's MTU MB 838 engine, giving a power/weight ratio of 18.2hp/t.[12] The Renk HWSL-284-C fully automatic hydromechanical transmission is used, with four forward and two reverse gears providing a maximum road speed of 61km/h. It is equipped with an electronic monitoring system and a transmission control system, and is capable of neutral steering. The engine and transmission are mounted in the front of the hull, as is typical for modern SPGs, to the left and front of the driver; both units are combined into a single

Powerpack of a PzH 2000NL. Modern Western AFVs usually combine their engines and transmissions into a single unit that can be quickly replaced with the help of an armoured recovery vehicle. This was never done for Soviet vehicles and is still not used by most modern Russian AFVs. (Alf van Beem)

powerpack for quick replacement. The torsion bar suspension has seven road wheels. It contains elements from both the Leopard 1 and 2 MBTs: for example, the road wheels are taken from the Leopard 2. Five telescopic hydraulic shock absorbers are used on the three front and two rear suspension units on each side. The suspension is normally covered by reinforced rubber side skirts, but these are often removed in the field. The tracks are of the double-pin 'live' type with rubber pads.[13] The Ukrainians have reported that they do not perform well in mud, which is a significant problem in Ukraine during the spring and fall *bezdorizhzhia* muddy seasons.[14] In addition to the engine, the PzH 2000 has a 1.9kW one-cylinder diesel APU, mounted on the left rear of the hull over the tracks. The PzH 2000 is very dependent on electrical power for its extensive automated systems, but the APU has proven less reliable than desired and Rheinmetall has been tasked with developing a replacement.[15]

Context

In Western and even Russian defence circles, the PzH 2000 has sometimes been hailed as the 'most advanced SPG in the world'; the gold standard by which all other SPGs are to be compared.[16,17] The Russo-Ukrainian War marks the first real test of the system in high-intensity warfare: the first PzH 2000s arrived in Ukraine in June 2022, seven PzH 2000 A1 from Germany and five PzH 2000NL from the Netherlands. At the time of writing, 28 systems are known

PzH 2000 of 43 Art. with side skirts removed, giving a good view of the suspension. (Arsenii Gerasymenko)

to have been delivered to Ukraine, and as far as is publicly known, they are concentrated in two artillery brigades: 26 Art. and 43 Art. The former also uses the Polish *Krab* SPG, which will be the subject of the next section. In the latter, they serve together with the *Pion*, already described in the preceding volume.

When compared to Soviet-legacy or Russian SPGs, the PzH 2000 has many significant advantages, at least on paper. The only Soviet/Russian system that can match or exceed its L/52 barrel in terms of range without resorting to assisted projectiles is the *Pion*, which is in turn significantly inferior to the PzH 2000 in terms of rate-of-fire, reaction time, displacement time, survivability, and fire control. It also lacks any type of smart munition. The *Msta*-SM2 is probably the closest Russian equivalent to the PzH 2000 in terms of fire control, although it is substantially outranged by the German SPG and lacks its survivability features. Modern Western SPGs generally are quite comparable to the PzH 2000 in terms of fire control and reaction time, as most feature some sort of advanced FCS paired with INS/SNS with datalinks for command and control. However, according to the PzH 2000's chief designer Frank Abels, no other Western SPG has 'true' MRSI capability: they can 'only' do three-round MRSI instead of five-round MRSI of the PzH 2000.[18] Western competitors to the PzH 2000 also generally lack its level of automation and survivability features.

Does the PzH 2000 live up to its reputation in Ukraine? That question will be answerable in full only after the war is over, given the lack of publicly available data. However, what little there is in the public sphere may perhaps suggest a few things that stand out. The first is that the survivability features incorporated into the PzH 2000 appear to be very effective. Despite numerous videos of PzH 2000s being hit or near-missed by counterbattery fire or *Lantset* loitering munitions posted by the Russians, there has not been a visually confirmed destruction of a PzH 2000 at the time of writing. In August 2024, the German newspaper *Frankfurter Allgemeine Zeitung* (FAZ) visited a PzH 2000 crew operating near Toretsk. They stated that there are plenty of videos showing their SPG being hit or near-missed; it was even hit once in the charge compartment but remained operational, the crew expressing their appreciation for its excellent protection.[19] Other Ukrainian crews have also complimented the level of automation and speed at which the PzH 2000 can complete its tasks, enabling it to easily outshoot any of the older Soviet SPGs Ukrainian forces have previously used and that still form the bulk of the Russian artillery arm.[20]

On the other hand, we also have evidence that the Ukrainians are not able to use the PzH 2000 to its full potential due to a combination of circumstantial factors. In the same FAZ article, the Ukrainian crew indicated that they are severely lacking in spare parts for the SPG, which forces them to cannibalise parts from other PzH 2000s and means that not all the SPGs can be operational at once. This is exacerbated by the complex electronics and automated systems of the PzH 2000, which are quite maintenance-intensive and can be sensitive to moisture in the environment; the Ukrainians are not able to provide luxurious climate-controlled storage for their PzH 2000s like the *Bundeswehr* can for its units.[21] The Ukrainians are also short on 155mm ammunition, and are thus not able to take advantage of features like the MRSI capability as they have to ration the shells. However, both of these are results of the relatively lackadaisical approach that the European nations have taken in retooling their military-industrial complexes to arm Ukraine and set up the infrastructure to support the SPGs, not inherent flaws of the PzH 2000.

Nevertheless, there is little doubt that the PzH 2000 has proved itself to be a very capable system when fully functioning and supported. The Ukrainians, at one point, considered buying up to 100 SPGs from Germany, but there is a very big question mark over whether the Ukrainian logistical system could sustain such a large force of these complex systems: this may have been why they have not followed through with the order at the time of writing.[22] These are not necessarily weaknesses inherent in the design of the PzH 2000, but it does underline a critically important lesson that has been repeatedly taught by military history: a weapon is only as strong as the rest of the system (especially logistics) that supports it. The Ukrainians have to determine if they want to invest their resources in the infrastructure needed to be able to field this potentially formidable system in the numbers needed to have a decisive impact on the war.

Germany has committed to delivering another 20 PzH 2000s to Ukraine from both Bundeswehr and industry stocks at the time of writing. It will also provide the Boxer RCH 155, which utilises the same gun in an automated turret on a wheeled platform. (Arsenii Gerasymenko)

GUIDED & CLUSTER MUNITIONS

Artillery has traditionally been an area weapon, often requiring large expenditures of ammunition in order to achieve a destructive effect on a target or inflict casualties. For example, during the Vietnam War, the US Army found that it took on average 13.7 155mm M107 conventional HE shells to achieve a kill, while a live demonstration using 24 vehicle targets saw the expenditure of 432 M107 shells achieving only eight hits in total.[23] The dispersion of conventional artillery shells also increases with range as errors and dispersion due to various factors are magnified, e.g. 155mm M795 HE has a circular error of probability (CEP) of 119m at 20km, while M549 RAP has a CEP of 286m at 30km. The quest for more lethality has therefore led to two approaches for improving the efficiency of artillery: guided munitions and cluster munitions.

The first artillery PGM to enter service was the American 155mm M712 Copperhead in 1981.[24][25] It remains in service today and is known to have been supplied to Ukraine. Copperhead was designed to destroy hardened point targets such as tanks and bunkers using a shaped charge warhead. It employs semi-active laser-homing guidance: a nose-mounted seeker guides the projectile using its fins based on laser reflections from a laser designator off of the target during the terminal homing phase. This guidance method is also preferred for Soviet and Russian cannon-launched PGMs, the most common of which is the *Krasnopol* family of 152mm PGMs. However, it requires a forward observer equipped with a laser designator (e.g. UAS or ground spotter team), and bad visibility conditions (e.g. heavy cloud cover, fog, smoke) can heavily degrade the accuracy of such projectiles. The laser can also alert the target if it is equipped with laser warning receivers.

Since the end of the Cold War, Western militaries have generally preferred GPS-guided PGMs for attacking stationary targets and sensor-fused munition (SFM) projectiles against armour. Arguably the most well-known example of the former is the rocket-assisted American-Swedish 155mm M982 Excalibur (see M777 section). Another known to be used by Ukraine is the Italian Vulcano 155 sub-calibre long-range (up to 70km from 155mm L/52) projectile, which comes in GPS-guided (GLR) and unguided (BER) variants.[26] It can also be equipped with a laser-

Top: 155 BONUS round cross-section. The SFM detonation (lower left) converts the metal liner into a lethal high-velocity slug traveling at over 2,000m/s. This Russian T-90M (lower right) was hit by one such SFM and immediately began burning due to the ammunition stored in the autoloader carousel magazine cooking off. (US Army; Bofors; Hinla Chereshnia)

Ukrainian L119 Light Gun No. 51054, 79th Air Assault Brigade, May 2024. It appears that L119s donated by the UK and Australia have been distributed to Ukraine's Air Assault Forces, while M119s have gone to the Ground Forces. (Artwork by David Bocquelet)

Ukrainian M777A2 'Meri' in its deployed configuration, 406th Artillery Brigade, October 2022. The barrel bears the inscription 'From Scotland'. (Artwork by David Bocquelet)

Ukrainian M1083 Medium Tactical Vehicle (MTV) with B-kit cabin add-on armour towing an M777A2 howitzer, 406th Artillery Brigade, October 2022. Based on an Austrian Steyr design modified and built by Oshkosh, the MTV is the prime mover for the M777. It is from the same Family of Medium Tactical Vehicles (FMTV) that includes the M1140 High Mobility Artillery Rocket System (HIMARS). (Artwork by David Bocquelet)

Ukrainian M109A3GN, September 2022. M109A3GNs are German M109Gs sold to Norway and subsequently modernised. Most were retired from Norwegian service prior to 2022 and donated to Ukraine after the invasion. (Artwork by David Bocquelet)

Ukrainian M109A5Ö, 92nd Assault Brigade, December 2023. The inscription says '*Boritesia-poborete! Vam Bog pomogae*' ('Struggle on—and be triumphant! God Himself will aid you'), which are lines from the Ukrainian poet Taras Shevchenko's poem '*Kavkaz*'. (Artwork by David Bocquelet)

Ukrainian M109A6 Paladin, 47th Mechanised Brigade, July 2024. This unit spearheaded the unsuccessful Ukrainian summer 2023 counteroffensive; it was formed in 2022 using exclusively American AFVs like the M1 Abrams and M2 Bradley and thus lacked combat experience, but has since matured into one of the more effective Ukrainian brigades. (Artwork by David Bocquelet)

Ukrainian M109A6 Paladin 'Poliana', 118th Mechanised Brigade, July 2024. Most Paladins have had their .50 M2HB heavy machine guns removed, as the Ukrainians do not find the weapon useful on an SPG and consider it a hindrance. (Artwork by David Bocquelet)

Ukrainian M992 Field Artillery Ammunition Supply Vehicle (FAASV), 47th Mechanised Brigade. FAASVs were designed to 'dock' with the rear doors of M109s to supply them with ammunition, but the Ukrainians appear to have found them to be too conspicuous for ammunition resupply in combat positions. (Artwork by David Bocquelet)

Ukrainian AS90, 3rd Assault Brigade, April 2024. This unit was formed in 2023 from Azov Rgt. units that were outside of Mariupol during the 2022 siege. This unit (as well as the NHU's Azov Brigade) has attracted controversy due to the far-right views expressed by some of their personnel, but it is considered one of the most combat effective Ukrainian units. (Artwork by David Bocquelet)

Ukrainian *Krab*, 26th Artillery Brigade, October 2023. Since 2022, the brigade has retired its *Msta*-S and *Giatsint*-S SPGs in favour of *Krabs*. It also operated PzH 2000s at one point. White crosses are a common identification marking for Ukrainian vehicles. (Artwork by David Bocquelet)

Ukrainian PzH 2000 'Tina', 43rd Artillery Brigade, February 2023. This is one of only two units known to have operated the PzH 2000, the other being the 26th Artillery Brigade. The Ukrainians often remove the side skirts from their PzH 2000s, likely to ease access for maintenance. (Artwork by David Bocquelet)

Ukrainian CAESAR, May 2022. CAESARs sent to Ukraine directly from French military arsenals had the standard green-black-brown French camouflage. (Artwork by David Bocquelet)

Ukrainian CAESAR, 55th Artillery Brigade, June 2024. This CAESAR has its identification cross made using white tape. New-build vehicles for Ukraine like this one (built in 2023) are uniform green instead of camouflaged. (Artwork by David Bocquelet)

Bohdana prototype on KrAZ-63221 chassis, as seen during the Battle for Zmiinyi Island, June 2022. The prototype had been stored in Kramatorsk and was dismantled to prevent capture during the early stages of the 2022 Russian invasion. It was saved by Serhiy Pashynskyi, who had the parts transported to Zhytomyr and reassembled. (Artwork by David Bocquelet)

Bohdana on Tatra Phoenix 8x8 chassis, 47th Artillery Brigade, February 2024. This is the latest version of the *Bohdana* SPG known to be in service. The armoured cab, produced by the Ukrainian Armor company, is based on their *Novator* infantry mobility vehicle. (Artwork by David Bocquelet)

Ukrainian *Dana*, 110th Mechanised Brigade, November 2023. It was destroyed near Avdiivka in February 2024. This is the only unit known to operate original *Danas*, donated by Czechia after the 2022 invasion. (Artwork by David Bocquelet)

Ukrainian M120K *Rak* 'Shuravi', 44th Mechanised Brigade, February 2023. Based on the Polish *Rosomak* 8x8 wheeled APC, *Rak* has an advanced FCS and autoloader, allowing it to open fire within 30 seconds, fire six to eight bombs/minute, and displace in 15 seconds. An undisclosed number have been provided by Poland to Ukraine. (Artwork by David Bocquelet)

Ukrainian 130 K 54, September 2023. Finland bought these guns (130mm M-46s) from the USSR during the Cold War, literally exchanging guns for (surplus) butter. These were retired in 2019, and Finland has donated an undisclosed number to Ukraine. (Artwork by David Bocquelet)

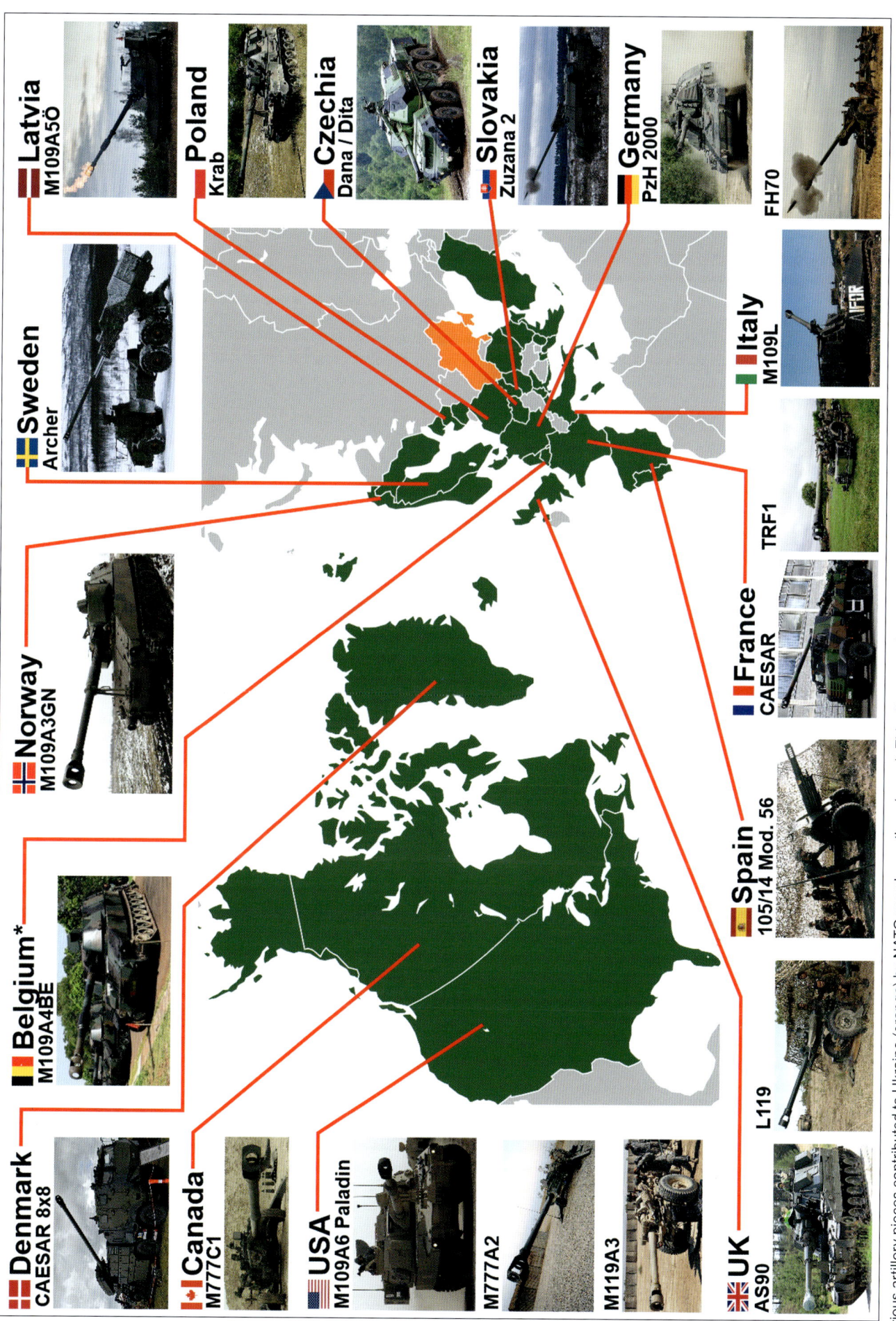

Various artillery pieces contributed to Ukraine (orange) by NATO member nations (green). This diagram only shows weapons according to the supplying country and is not meant a complete list. Some (e.g. PzH 2000) have been donated by more than one country (Germany, the Netherlands, and Italy), but duplicates are not shown. Many other NATO member nations contribute ammunition and other supplies. Soviet-legacy weapons donated by these nations are also not shown. *Ex-Belgian M109A4BEs were purchased from the private company FTS by the UK and donated to Ukraine. (Author's diagram)

Top: *Kropyva* tablet being held up by a Ukrainian artilleryman with a *Pion* SPG in the background. Bottom: *Kropyva*'s interface, as seen running on a Windows desktop during the NATO Dynamic Front 2020 exercise. *Kropyva* is a mapping software that is primarily used as a ballistic calculator and situational awareness too. It is also capable of functioning as a battlefield management system. *Kropyva* is designed to run on Android systems, thus an Android emulator such as NoxPlayer is required for Windows PCs. (ArmySOS; 26 Art.)

homing head instead of the programmable fuse for terminal laser guidance and improved precision.[27] GPS PGMs have the advantage of not needing a forward designator; once the target coordinates are inputted and the projectile is fired, it will use GPS navigation signals to guide itself to the target without any external intervention. Unfortunately, they are also vulnerable to GPS jamming: Excalibur's hit rate in Ukraine reportedly dropped from 55 percent to only six percent once the Russians began deploying their electronic warfare systems.[28] Ukrainian artillerymen the author has spoken to consistently state that GPS jamming has mostly nullified Excalibur.

Artillery SFM projectiles dispense SFMs, i.e. submunitions that search for their own targets autonomously. Two examples of such projectiles used by Ukrainian forces are the Franco-Swedish BONUS and German DM702 SMArt 155.[29] Both are similar in that they employ two explosively formed penetrator (EFP) SFMs that are released from the shell at a predetermined height above a target area, though BONUS's shell has a BB tail section for longer range. The SFMs will then descend slowly: using winglets to slow down while autorotating akin to a sycamore maple seed for BONUS; by parachute for SMArt 155. As they descend, they search for a target using their onboard sensors: ladar for BONUS; millimetric wave radar and IR sensor for SMArt.[30, 31] Once the SFM detects a target within the EFP warhead's effective range, it detonates, sending a high-velocity metal slug into the target's roof to disable/destroy it. BONUS's manufacturer datasheet claims that its SFM can penetrate up to 140mm of RHA. SFMs have proven to be highly effective against Russian tanks in Ukraine, as they feature an autoloader ammunition magazine in a circular arrangement under the turret, providing a large target for SFMs striking from above with potentially catastrophic results.[32, 33] Explosive reactive armour (ERA) and add-on slat armour are mostly ineffective against EFPs, as they generally do not trigger ERA explosives and can simply punch through the slats. They are also completely unaffected by electronic countermeasures.

In addition to guided shells, the US also pioneered the use of cluster shells: unguided shells which scatter unguided submunitions over a wide area. In a conventional shell, most of the damage from blast and fragmentation is concentrated near the hit area, quickly diminishing with distance. A cluster shell allows the damage to be spread out over a wide area, reducing the 'overkill' effect near the hit area and increasing the likelihood of a target being hit. The first generation using fragmentation submunitions known as improved conventional munitions (ICMs) were used in Vietnam, where it was found that they dramatically reduced the number of 155mm rounds per kill from 13.6 to 1.7. Second generation US cluster shells (e.g. M483A1 and M864) carry dozens of dual-purpose ICMs (DPICMs) with shaped charge-fragmentation warheads to increase their lethality against vehicles. These were provided to Ukraine by the US starting in the summer of 2023 (it is claimed but officially denied that Turkey had started supplying some of its own as early as November 2022), where they are proving to be highly effective on the battlefield.[34] The Soviets also had their own cluster shells equivalent to US ICM/DPICM shells (see the previous volume's projectile table), and these

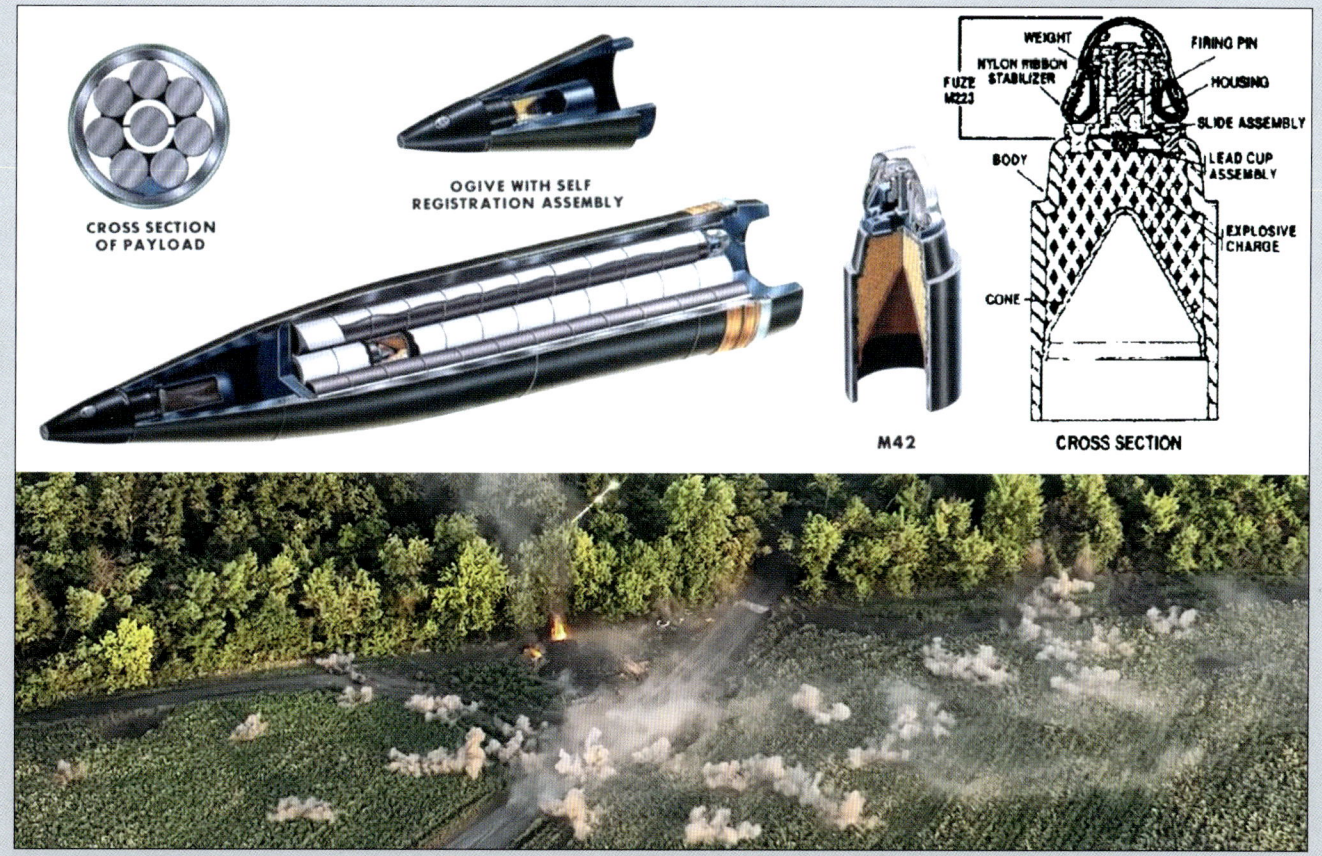

Illustrative cross-section of an M483A1 DPICM shell. Top right: cross-section of an M42 DPICM impact-fused grenade. The shaped charge can penetrate ~70 mm of RHA, while the body is pre-fragmented to shatter into small fragments upon detonation. One shell carries 88 DPICMs, which are scattered in the air before detonating on impact with the ground (bottom). Ground-burst DPICMs can be effective against personnel in the open, but their effectiveness is strongly affected by terrain. (US Army; 47 Mech.)

are used by both sides of the war. Additionally, mine-dispersal shells such as the American M692/M731 ADAM (Area Denial Artillery Munition) and M718A1/M741A1 RAAMS (Remote Anti-Armor Mine Systems) are also being used in Ukraine. These munitions scatter limited lifespan anti-personnel and anti-armour mines to create temporary minefields to restrict the movements of enemy forces, either slowing them down or forcing them on to terrain favourable to the user.

Guided and cluster shells are very useful supplements to conventional shells, but they cannot be expected to be complete replacements due to the relatively small number produced. The former are much more expensive than conventional shells, and their larger length also means that SPGs usually have to carry them in special racks, thus restricting the amount carried. Cluster shell submunitions can fail to detonate or self-destruct, leaving behind unexploded ordnance that can become a threat to civilians long after the conflict ends; thus, their use is somewhat controversial. It should also be noted that the comparisons given earlier are for M107, a very old HE shell design dating back to the Second World War: modern HE shells with thin casings and more filler can match or exceed the lethal area of cluster shells, at least in terms of anti-personnel fragmentation. Ukraine, the US, and Russia have not signed the Convention on Cluster Munitions, which restricts the use and transfer of cluster munitions, including cluster artillery shells. Ukraine is, however, a signatory of the Ottawa Treaty banning the use of anti-personnel mines (the US and Russia are non-signatories). Despite this, faced with relentless Russian infantry-centric infiltration and massed attacks, Ukraine has asked for and received ADAMs from the US starting in November 2024.[35]

5
AS90 & *KRAB*: A MARRIAGE OF CONVENIENCE

AS90

Development History

While the British Army was saddled with the troubled trinational SP70 SPG project throughout the 1980s, VSEL was working on its own 155mm SPG as a private venture for the export market. They had already designed a modular 155mm artillery turret intended to be mounted on an existing MBT chassis called GBT-155 in 1982, and this would be the starting point for their new SPG project. They realised that an unmodified MBT chassis was ill-suited to the SPG role due to the lack of space, excessive weight, and suboptimal turret location for ammunition resupply (as the SP70 developers were also finding out), thus their new SPG would need a dedicated chassis. To this end, VSEL collaborated with the British Cummins (powerpack) and Brazilian Verolme Estaleiros Reunidos do Brazil (chassis) companies on what was initially called the V²C ('Vickers — Verolme — Cummins') SPG; VSEL itself would be responsible for the turret (essentially GBT-155 modified with a larger turret ring) and armament.

The new SPG's design emphasised several key features: ease of operation, reliability, modular construction to fit any possible customer's requirements, and accuracy and rate-of-fire that matched the FH70 towed howitzer. Customers would be able to choose different features as desired, such as the loading system (assisted or fully automatic) or the armament (155mm L/39, L/45, and even L/52 options were offered). The first prototype was completed in 1986 with an L/39 barrel, by which time its name had been changed to 'AS90' ('Artillery System 90'[1]).[2] That same year, the SP70 project finally imploded and the British Army were now looking for proposals to replace it. VSEL submitted a modified variant, AS90B, and it emerged as the winner in 1989 after competitive trials, with 179 ordered by the British government. The AS90 was thus adopted by the British Army in 1992 to replace both the Abbot and M109 SPGs.[3] Although it was assigned the L-number designation 'L131', it is almost universally referred to as 'AS90' in British service. By this time, Verolme had gone bankrupt, leaving VSEL and Cummins to continue with the partnership.[4]

Ironically, despite being originally designed for the export market, the AS90 as a whole has not achieved any export success. Verolme was to market the AS90 to developing countries, but their bankruptcy put paid to this. The AS90 also faced stiff competition from the 'gold-plated' PzH 2000 at the upper end of the market and cheaper M109 upgrades at the lower end, thus it was squeezed out of the export market. In the 1990s, it was planned to upgrade the British AS90s with the 155mm L/52 Extended-Range Ordnance (ERO) and modular charges, but this was cancelled before any were upgraded.[5] Upgrades have thus mostly been limited to the fire control and communications equipment. The AS90 with ERO was offered along with desert modifications on the export market as the 'AS90 Braveheart'.[6] It was also offered as a modular turret like the GBT-155, and in this form, the AS90 did eventually find one export customer: Poland, who bought the production licence and equipment for the AS90 Braveheart turret system to use with the *Krab* SPG, as will be seen later.

Since January 2023, Britain has sent a significant fraction of its AS90s to Ukraine as aid. These have received upgrades over their 30+ years of service, thus some of the technical and equipment fit information from older sources such as Forecast International's Military Vehicles Forecast (1999) or Armada International (1990) is outdated. Relatively little official or authoritative technical literature has been publicly released on the AS90: the author has attempted, to the best of their ability, to cross-reference the older sources with newer sources to provide information on the AS90s as they have been sent to Ukraine.

Technical Summary

The AS90 is armed with a 155mm L31 ordnance with an L/39 monobloc autofrettaged barrel. This weapon is fitted with a double-baffle muzzle brake and features what is known as a 'split-block breech'. This is a vertical sliding-block breech with an obturator

AS90 of the 117th Mechanised Brigade operating on the Pokrovsk front, December 2024. Shorter ranged SPGs in Ukraine tend to operate from camouflaged or entrenched positions like this (located only 7km from Russian positions) to avoid detection, emerging and moving only short distances from these positions to fire. (ArmyInform)

mushroom head built into the breech block: when the breech is closed, the obturator moves horizontally into place to seal off the propellant gases in the barrel during firing.[7] It also contains a 12-round primer magazine, allowing the use of bagged propellant charges with the faster action benefits of a sliding-block breech.[8] The loading system attached to the gun consists of two projectile trays, one on a shell transfer arm and the other with a flick rammer. It is designed to provide a three-round burst: with one round already in breech, the AS90 can load and fire the next two shells in quick succession within 10 seconds. Six rounds/minute can be maintained for three minutes, with two rounds/minute sustained. Charges are loaded manually.[9]

The turret bustle contains two mechanised conveyor magazines for 31 projectiles, with a feeder mechanism in between to send shells to the shell transfer arm of the loading mechanism. Due to the asymmetric layout, the right magazine holds 21 projectiles, the left

AS90 of 116 Mech. firing at Russian targets, October 2024. Ukrainian crews have generally spoken positively about the AS90's fire control capabilities. (United24)

Top left: AS90 loaders' station. Top right: the loading system can be seen with a projectile on its shell transfer arm to the left. Bottom: AS90 loading sequence. After the first round is fired, the next projectile in the flick rammer's tray directly behind the breech is raised to the loading line and rammed. The projectile in the second tray is then moved to the now-empty flick rammer tray and a charge is inserted manually. The process is then repeated for the last projectile. (3 Assault)

holds 10. Twenty-one charges are stored above the projectiles, with another 10 on the front left of the turret. Another 17 projectiles and charges are stored in the hull for a total of 48 each.[10] Ammunition management is done through the Turret Control Computer (TCC), which also manages the turret drives. British AS90s, as sent to Ukraine, have the LINAPS (Laser Inertial Artillery Pointing System) with integrated FIN3110 INS/SNS for automated gun-laying.[11] An Avimo DFS90 day/night telescopic sight is also fitted for direct fire; it is also used for indirect fire if the LINAPS fails.[12] The commander also has an image intensifier day/night sight. The gun can be elevated up to 70° and the turret provides full 360° traverse using electric drives. The standard radio fitted is the Bowman type in a box on the lower left turret rear.[13]

The exact armour thicknesses of the AS90 are not publicly known, but it is claimed to be up to 17mm thick and can 'stop fragments from a very near burst of a 155mm shell or small arms fire at point blank range'.[14, 15] A 7.62mm L7 GPMG (general-purpose machine gun) is fitted on the loader's hatch, with 1,000 rounds provided. Ten smoke grenade launchers are mounted on the turret face in clusters of five on each side of the gun. The AS90 in British service nominally has a six-man crew onboard, but Ukrainian units operate them with a smaller crew of five: driver, commander, gunner, and two loaders. The AS90 can be made ready to fire within one minute with a well-trained crew.[16]

The 45t AS90 is powered by a Cummins 669hp VTA-903T-660 liquid-cooled 4-stroke V-8 diesel engine providing a power/weight ratio of 14.9hp/t. The Zahnradfabrik Friedrichshafen (ZF) LSG 2000 automatic transmission has four forward and two reverse gears, providing a maximum road speed of 55km/h. The combined powerpack is mounted in the forward part of the hull, left of the driver, and can be replaced in an hour by trained mechanics and the assistance of an armoured recovery vehicle (ARV).[17] A Horstman Hydrogas external suspension is used. It consists of individual hydropneumatic suspension units that use high pressure nitrogen gas as the spring element instead of torsion bars and an integral oil damper, and is the type favoured by the British and used on many of their modern AFVs such as the Challenger MBTs as it eliminates the hull space taken by torsion bars and is easier to replace when damaged.[18] The AS90 also has a Cummins 2-stroke diesel engine for an APU, located in the forward part of the hull.[19]

Krab

Development History

As a former Warsaw Pact member, the Polish military (WP, *Wojsko Polskie*) was mostly equipped with Soviet or Warsaw Pact weapons, including 152mm artillery such as the *Dana* (see the chapter on the *Dana* family). As early as 1993, the Polish manufacturer Huta Stalowa Wola (HSW) proposed to the Polish General Staff the idea of collaborating with the Slovak state company KONŠTRUKTA Defence to adapt their new *Zuzana* 155mm wheeled SPG's turret to the tracked chassis of the *Kalina* minelayer (itself a joint

AS90s from 116 Mech., October (top) and August (bottom) 2024. The original AS90 did not have return rollers, visible here under the sideskirt. The crew of the top AS90 expressed that the tracks were inadequate for the Ukrainian muddy season during an interview. (United24; 116 Mech.)

East German-Polish project based on the Soviet MT-S tracked transporter). This idea was met with approval and marked the beginning of the *Zuzanna* project.[20]

The *Zuzanna* project called for the selection of a turret to be mounted on the *Kalina*-based SPG. After several false starts, the Polish MON (*Ministerstwo Obrony Narodowej*, Ministry of National Defence) selected the British AS90 Braveheart with the 155mm L/52 ERO to arm the new SPG in 1999.[21] As the British Army was no longer ordering new AS90s (the 'peace dividend'), the AS90 turret production licence as well as all the production equipment was sold to Poland. That same year, Poland would join the NATO alliance, and thus there was increased interest in procuring NATO-compliant 155mm systems. The OBRUM (*Ośrodek Badawczo-Rozwojowy Urządzeń Mechanicznych*, Research and Development Centre for Mechanical Devices) research institute worked on the new SPG chassis, now called 'UPG-NG' (*Uniwersalne Podwozie Gąsienicowe – Nowej Generacji*, Universal Tracked Chassis – Next Generation). It now used the suspension elements and engine of the PT-91 *Twardy* MBT, which is itself a derivative of the Soviet T-72 MBT. In 2000, the MON signed a contract with HSW to develop the new SPG, now codenamed '*Krab*'.[22, 23]

The first prototype *Krab* based on the UPG-NG chassis was finished in 2001 and successfully completed trials in 2003, with mass production planned to begin that year. However, financial cutbacks and political controversy would severely delay things, and it was not until 2006 that the MON would order the *Krab* into production alongside the *Azalia* battery command and *Waran* ammunition resupply vehicles: these vehicles were intended to operate together as the *Regina* artillery battalion fires module. In the meantime, more problems appeared: Britain had stopped producing AS90 barrels and a replacement had to be sought. Initially, the Poles settled on a French Nexter design from the Atelier de Construction de Bourges, then bought some German barrels from Rheinmetall for the SPGs of the first *Regina* module; it was not until 2016 that HSW was able to start producing its own barrels for the *Krab*, completing the process of 'Polonising' the AS90 turret. The first *Regina* module was delivered to the WP in 2012, but this was not to be the end of the *Krab*'s troubles. Severe defects were found in the planned serial UPG-NG chassis produced by the Bumar-Łabędy factory during testing, such as microcracks and insufficient cooling for its S-12U engine. The S-12U engine itself became another source for headaches when its manufacturer PZL-Wola was liquidated and a new replacement had to be sought.[24]

These problems nearly led to the collapse of the *Krab* programme and were only finally resolved in 2014 when the decision was made to use the chassis of the Korean K9 Thunder SPG with a German MTU diesel engine.[25] The story of the K9's development and how it has grown to become the dominant SPG on today's global arms

Krab of an unidentified Ukrainian artillery brigade, November 2023. Note the different hull and muzzle brake for the L/52 gun. (ArmyInform)

ROK Army K9 during the ROK Armed Forces 65th Anniversary Parade in Seoul, October 2013. The K9 has enjoyed remarkable export success and appears set to become the M109's successor as the 'standard' SPG of the Western world. Its chassis is used by the *Krab* and is built under licence in Poland. (Korea.net)

market is a most fascinating one, but unfortunately lies beyond the scope of this book as the system is not used in Ukraine at the time of writing; this section is already long enough as it is. Thus, the author must regrettably leave it for others to tell. Suffice to say, the K9's manufacturer, Hanwha Techwin, was able to offer their proven chassis with technology transfer on terms that were too good for the Poles pass up. Thus, this marriage of the AS90 Braveheart turret, K9 Thunder chassis, and German MTU engine was finally consecrated into service as the serial production version of the *Krab*. Production has been completely localised in Poland since 2020.[26]

Technical Summary

The *Krab* uses a 'Polonised' AS90 Braveheart turret: the author was informed by Antoni Walkowski, an editor at Polish defence publication Defense24, that the turret has been sufficiently localised to the point where HSW no longer needs to pay licensing fees to BAE, VSEL's successor. In terms of capabilities and general characteristics it is very similar to the AS90's turret, the biggest difference being the use of the 155mm ERO with L/52 barrel instead of L/39 on British AS90s. Like on the AS90, the gun is fed by a loading system with a flick rammer that allows for a 3-round burst in 10 seconds; the turret ammunition stowage arrangement is similar (though it has been reduced to 29 projectiles and 28 charges). Unlike British AS90s, the *Krab* has been adapted to use modular charges.[27]

The fire control is integrated with the Polish *Topaz* artillery BMS; it includes a Polish DD9620 ballistic computer and American Honeywell TALIN 5000 INS/SNS mated to the 'Polonised' AS90 TCC controlling the turret mechanisms.[28] The *Krab* can thus open fire within 30 seconds of coming to a stop. The communications suite consists of the domestic FONET intercom and RRC 9311AP radio set. Another change is the use of a 12.7mm WKM-B (Polish variant of the Soviet *Utyos* AAMG firing NATO .50 BMG cartridges) instead of the L7 GPMG on the loader's hatch. The *Krab* also has only eight smoke grenade launchers instead of 10 on the turret face. Presumably, the turret armour is the same as on the AS90 (17mm RHA max), but this remains to be confirmed. There is provision for the Obra-3 SSP-1 laser warning system, but this does not seem to be fitted to Ukrainian *Krabs*.

The *Krab* utilises the K9 SPG chassis with modifications to suit Polish requirements, designated 'PK9'. It is made from steel RHA plate, and is resistant against 14.5mm bullets and artillery shrapnel.[29] Eleven projectiles and 20 charges are also stored in the hull. The *Krab*'s combat weight is 48t, and it is powered by a 1,000 hp MTU MT881Ka-500 liquid-cooled V-8 diesel engine licence-built in the ROK by STX Engine, providing a power/weight ratio of 20.8hp/t. This is combined with an Allison X1100-5A3 hydromechanical automatic transmission (four forward, two reverse gears) in a forward-mounted powerpack, giving a maximum road speed of 60km/h. A hydropneumatic suspension is used, with six road wheels and three return rollers on each side and rubber-padded dual-pin tracks. In addition, unlike the original K9, the *Krab* has a 5.5kW APU mounted on the right rear hull and an NBC filter/ventilation system on the left rear hull.

Context

Ukraine began receiving *Krabs* in May 2022, and at least 72 units have been donated by Poland with a further 54 ordered by Ukraine. These have been sent together with *Azalia* battery command vehicles, which allow the *Krabs* to be used to their full potential via the *Topaz* BMS's datalink and *Krabs*' automated gun-laying system. They were subsequently followed by AS90s from Britain, of which at least 70 operational units have been donated together with 12 non-functional units intended as spares. This represents nearly half of the British Army's AS90s.[30] As far as can be seen from publicly available information, *Krabs* have been reserved for Ukrainian artillery brigades, while the shorter-ranged AS90s have gone to

Krab firing at Russian forces, August 2022. The *Krab* has been praised by the Ukrainians for its high accuracy, reliability, and ease of use; a testament to the soundness of VSEL's original turret and gun design as well as the Polish defence industry's manufacturing capabilities. (ArmyTV)

(A) The Krab's loading system is very similar to the AS90's. Here the projectile magazine feeder can be seen: the loader pulls it out with a handle to allow the projectile to slide out into the shell transfer arm's tray. (B) The commander (right) and gunner's (left) display units can be seen. Like all modern Western SPGs, the *Krab* can automatically lay the gun using coordinates entered by the gunner. (C) The turret face of a *Krab*. (D) WKM-B AAMG. (ArmyInform; ArmyTV)

Polish technicians from the PGZ (*Polska Grupa Zbrojeniowa*) Serwis Orel assist Ukrainians in maintaining the (A) powerpack and (B) APU of a *Krab*, somewhere near the frontline. (C) Close-up view of the *Krab* suspension. (D) *Krab* from the side, illustrating its typical SPG configuration. (PGZ; ArmyTV)

AS90 of 117 Mech., July 2024. Although the AS90 failed to live up to VSEL's commercial expectations, it has proved itself in combat with British and now Ukrainian forces. (117 Mech.)

other units such as tank and mechanised brigades, similar to the M109. Combined, this constitutes a total of at least 142 operational SPGs, making the AS90/*Krab* the second most prolific Western SPG known to be in service with Ukraine at the time of writing.

Both the AS90 and *Krab* have been well-received by the Ukrainians, who consider them a major advance over the old Soviet SPGs they previously operated, especially in terms of accuracy, fire control, and ease of use.[31, 32] The *Krab*, in particular, enjoys a solid logistical support infrastructure developed by neighbouring Poland both inside and outside of Ukraine, which enables it to be much more easily serviced than PzH 2000s that have to be sent abroad to be repaired, sometimes even near the frontlines.[33] This enables far more of the former to be kept operational at once than the latter, even if they lack some of the latter's more advanced features such as 'true' MRSI capability and a lower rate-of-fire. However, it should be noted that both AS90 and *Krab* lack the survivability features of the PzH 2000, and this is reflected by the relatively high *Krab* losses (27 confirmed destroyed at the time of writing), second highest among Western SPGs in Ukrainian service.

The UK plans to retire the AS90 by 2032, to be replaced by the German Boxer RCH 155 wheeled SPG.[34] It is not inconceivable that they will send most (if not all) of the British Army's stocks to Ukraine as the need arises and the system is drawn down, thus the Russo-Ukrainian War may be the system's swansong. After the February 2022 invasion, Poland has started an arms buying spree as it seeks to rearm in the face of a more aggressive Russia. It not only intends to order more *Krabs* but also the K9PL ('Polonised' K9), to be produced with Korean assistance in parallel with the *Krab* due to HSW's limited production capacity.[35, 36] It therefore seems likely that Ukraine will be able to acquire more *Krabs* if the means and desire exist. Certainly, the *Krab*'s combat experience in Ukraine has proved that, despite its troubled development, the *Krab* has matured into a capable system. The feedback obtained from combat will doubtless be invaluable for determining future improvements to Poland's own artillery systems. Thus, VSEL's AS90 will probably live on for the foreseeable future in the *Krab*.

Krab of 26 Art. firing at Russian forces, January 2024. As loitering munitions such as *Lantset* and armed FPVs have become more prolific, both sides have increasingly equipped their AFVs with anti-drone cage armour to provide stand-off protection. *Krabs* are particularly vulnerable to such weapons because of the combustible charges stored near the roof of the turret bustle, which are more likely to be hit since they usually strike from above. (ArmyTV)

6
CAESAR: WAY OF THE FUTURE?

Development History

By the end of the Cold War, the *Armée de Terre* (French Army) was equipped with two 155mm artillery types: the *canon 155 tracté modèle* F1 ('155mm towed gun model F1', abbreviated TRF1) and the *canon 155 automoteur modèle* F1 ('155mm SPG model F1', abbreviated AUF1). The former primarily served with infantry divisions, the *Force d'action rapide* ('Rapid action force', FAR), and other expedition-oriented forces, while the latter, based on the AMX-30 MBT chassis, served with armoured and mechanised divisions.[1] The former also had limited SP capability, being able to move at ~10km/h using its APU with hydraulics to assist with emplacing and displacing the gun.[2] Both used L/39 barrels that provided a maximum range of 24km with unassisted projectiles and up to 32km with RAP.[3]

CAESAR named 'Fugasik' ('The Little Explosive') of an unidentified Ukrainian artillery unit, May 2023. (United24)

French AUF1s of the 40th Artillery Regiment participating in Operation Joint Endeavour, Bosnia-Herzegovina, 1996. The AUF1 was one of the first SPGs to feature fully automatic loading of both projectiles and charges, achieving eight rounds/minute. (DoD)

Meanwhile, the artillery group of the French defence conglomerate GIAT (*Groupement industriel des armements terrestres*, Industrial group for army weapons, later Nexter and today KNDS France) had found itself in dire financial straits with the dawn of the 'peace dividend' era and defence cutbacks. With no future prospect of French orders, its only hope for financial salvation was the export market, but the AUF1 was hampered in this respect by its use of non-NATO standard charges for its autoloader and the TRF1 faced stiff competition from the American M198, trinational FH70 towed howitzers, and other systems. Furthermore, NATO was now moving towards the L/52 barrel for 155mm artillery.[4] Internal tests attempting to mount such a barrel on the TRF1 were 'catastrophic' and the gun required a new recoil system, which GIAT found difficult to justify developing in its financial situation.[5]

Simultaneously, it turned out that the cost of the TRF1's APU and hydraulics alone were on the same order of magnitude as its prime mover, the Renault TRM 10000 truck. This led to a very logical question: if it costs roughly the same to move the gun 100km on its own power as to move it 500km with a truck, why not just mount the gun on a truck in the first place? GIAT's engineers soon sketched out this new concept: long-range L/52 gun, transportability in a Lockheed C-130 transport plane as a single unit, NBC protection for the crew cabin, and ergonomics at least equivalent to that of the TRF1. The new weapon was dubbed 'Camion equipé d'un système d'artillerie' ('Truck equipped with an artillery system'): CAESAR.[6] [7]

Despite initial objections by GIAT's artillery technical team that no truck chassis could possibly withstand the powerful recoil of a 155mm L/52 weapon, a technical solution was eventually found for this problem, as was a suitable truck chassis in the German Unimog U 2450 imported by Lohr Industrie (now Soframe). GIAT's strategic committee were soon convinced that the project was a winner: a new, innovative design that could be developed at a low cost to fill a perceived niche for light SPGs. The technology could even possibly be used to adapt an L/52 barrel to the TRF1. As such, the project was approved and the first prototype completed in under a year, in time to be exhibited at the 1994 Eurosatory defence expo.[8]

In order to stimulate foreign customer interest in CAESAR, the Ministère de la Défense purchased five systems in 2000 and announced their induction into the Armée de Terre (who would want to buy the system if its parent country will not?) for 'tactical experimentation', despite the fact that there had been no official interest in acquiring new 155mm systems previously. This led to the joke that 'CAESAR' stood for 'Canon acheté par effet de surprise par Alain Richard' ('Canon purchased by surprise effect of Alain Richard'; French Minister of Defence at the time). However, the Armée de Terre soon came to appreciate the CAESAR's high mobility

TRF1 in service with the NHU's Azov Brigade, July 2023. At least six of these ex-French Army guns were purchased by Ukraine from S2M-Equipment. The author's NHU acquaintance has personal experience with the system: 'a very good gun but complex and prone to breaking'. (NHU Azov)

Ukrainian CAESAR 8x8 (Tatra 517) at the 199th Air Assault Forces Training Centre. The 8x8 version is more heavily armoured, carries 36 rounds, and has greater off-road mobility than the standard 6x6 variant, but is too large to be transported by a C-130. Denmark has donated 19 of these to Ukraine after the 2022 invasion. (199 Training Centre)

and long range.⁹ Today, CAESAR has mostly replaced both the AUF1 and TRF1 in French service. Export orders were also soon coming in; without any real competitors, CAESAR has practically monopolised the market for light wheeled SPGs.

CAESAR's artillery system can be adapted to a wide variety of truck chassis depending on the customer's requirements. The *Armée de Terre* uses the French Renault Sherpa 5 6x6 truck as the base for its CAESARs. This is also the most common version in Ukrainian service, thus it will be the one described in the technical summary. Ukraine also operates some CAESAR 8x8s based on the heavier Czech Tatra 517 8x8 truck, but all of these were donated by Denmark from their existing arsenal.[10]

Technical Summary

CAESAR's 155mm L/52 gun is JBMoU-compliant, and, given identical ammunition, can achieve the same ranges as other much heavier tracked SPGs. The use of such a powerful weapon on a truck chassis requires some innovative solutions to prevent the gun's recoil damaging the chassis. This was accomplished by a '*faux châssis*', a reinforced frame on which the gun is mounted that redirects the recoil energy into the hydraulically deployed rear stabiliser's spades: these must be deployed before firing.[11] The gun itself is equipped with a double-baffle muzzle brake similar to that found on the TRF1 and AUF1, but unlike the latter two, it has a semi-automatic interrupted screw breech. The gun is also fitted with a semi-automatic loader for projectiles similar to the TRF1's and a breech primer magazine (14 primers). Charges are loaded manually. These allow for a maximum rate-of-fire of six rounds/minute. Eighteen projectiles and charges each are carried onboard in boxes behind the cab.

The gun has a maximum elevation of 66° and traverse of +/-48°. It is possible to depress the gun down to -3° for direct fire using an optical sight, but the cab blocks the gun from depressing enough against targets directly ahead of the CAESAR.[12] Aiming, fuse-setting, and loading are managed using the FAST-Hit computerised FCS with integral INS/SNS and datalink. The various control blocks are located at the rear of the vehicle around the gun, thus the crew must exit the vehicle in order to load and aim the gun. The primary control unit is the BIHM (*Boitier d'interface homme-machine*, Human-machine interface box), which stores and processes combat mission information and controls the gun via a touch screen. FAST-Hit was designed with modularity in mind and can be adapted to any artillery network; in Ukrainian usage this means it has been adapted to work with *Kropyva* instead of the French ATLAS. In a Nexter promotional video, CAESAR was shown to be able to open fire within 50 seconds of coming to halt, fire six rounds, and be ready to displace one minute 34 seconds after firing the first round.[13]

Ukrainian CAESAR firing at Russian forces, May 2022. One of the projectile storage boxes can be seen with its lid open. (MOU)

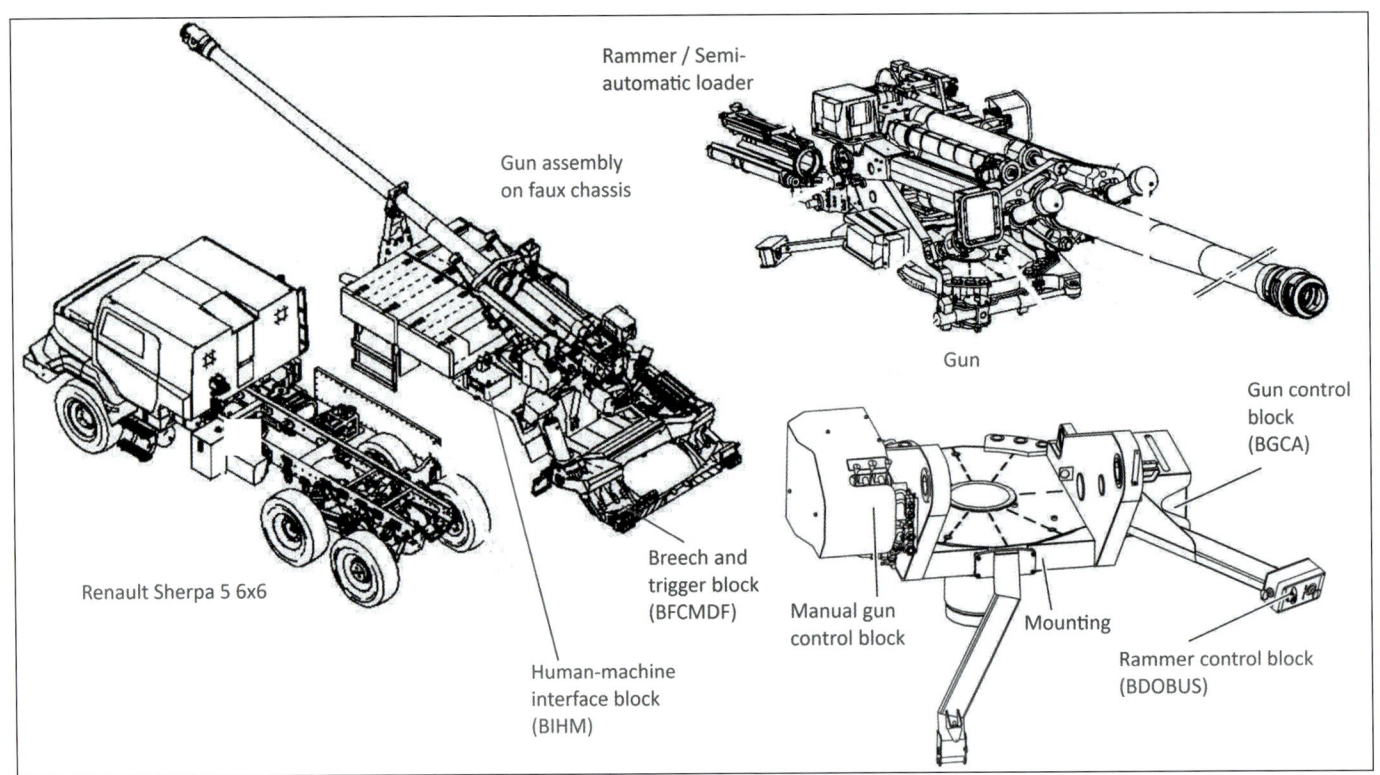

Illustrations from a Ukrainian CAESAR manual of the complete system (left), gun (upper right), and gun mounting (lower right). (Author's collection)

CAESAR, as currently used by Ukraine (excepting donated Danish CAESAR 8x8s), is based on the Renault Sherpa 5 6x6 tactical truck in its long-cab variant. The combat weight, including the gun and ammunition, is only 18.6t. The Sherpa 5 has a 240 hp Renault DXi 7 turbocharged six-cylinder inline 4-stroke diesel engine with air-air intercooling, providing a power/weight ratio of 12.9hp/t. The ZF 6S1000 mechanical synchromesh gearbox has six forward and one reverse gear (the automatic ZF 6HP602 gearbox is also available); paired with the VG 750-270 transfer box, it provides a top road speed of 80km/h. A Téléflow central tyre inflation system is also provided to improve cross-country performance.[14] The cab has space for the entire crew of five to be seated inside, which with the add-on armour kit provides STANAG 4569 Level 2 protection as well as NBC protection.

Context

In April 2022, France announced the first deliveries of CAESARs directly from *Armée de Terre* stocks, with the first systems sighted in Ukraine the following month.[15] At the time of writing there are 49 CAESARs known to have been delivered to Ukraine (including 19 CAESAR 8x8s donated by Denmark, its entire stock). Ukraine is set to receive at least another 30 in 2024, potentially up to 78 as part of a so-called 'artillery coalition' led by France and the US.[16] It is thus the third most common Western SPG used by Ukraine, after the M109 and *Krab*/AS90, based on known deliveries. Provided the funding exists, a lot more CAESARs can be expected in Ukrainian service in the future.

CAESAR in its traveling (left) and emplaced (right) configurations. On the left, one of the gunners can be seen using the BIHM control unit, while another prepares a shell for the semi-automatic loader. The button for firing the gun for the firing block (BFCMDF) can be seen just below the left hydraulic stabiliser unit: there is no provision to fire it from inside the cab. (MOU)

Ukrainian artillerymen prepare to emplace a CAESAR battery. The Russo-Ukrainian War marks the first real test of CAESAR in a high-intensity symmetric peer war, which it has passed with flying colours. (MOU)

CAESAR's primary selling points are its relatively low cost, simplicity, as well as high mobility. The former is particularly attractive for Ukraine, as that means they will be able to field more CAESARs and more easily sustain them for a given price. CAESAR relies on its mobility and long-range for survival: the truck only provides limited protection for the crew while seated inside the armoured cab, and they are completely exposed while operating the gun. The high *strategic* mobility from being mounted on a truck chassis allows them to be quickly redeployed to different sectors connected by road networks, while its *tactical* mobility on the actual battlefield under most conditions is as good as that of any cross-country 6x6 truck (though obviously more limited than for a tracked vehicle in bad terrain or mud). However, the Ukrainians, while generally quite satisfied with CAESAR, have also expressed some dissatisfaction with its reliability in rough conditions.[17]

Conversely, on a now-deleted Telegram channel, a Russian artilleryman gave his view of CAESAR:

Their most terrible weapon is the CAESAR. It is used to hit especially important targets and to counterbattery our guns. The firing range of a regular shell of more than 40km makes this weapon out of reach of return fire from our Soviet guns. We do not have such weapons, and even long-range shells fly 32km maximum. The wheelbase of this dickhead allows it to quickly get away from its position, even if it has already been exposed. It deploys in 60 seconds. It displaces in 40. The FCS is automated, which leads to fucking amazing accuracy. In general, this weapon is simply from another century compared to most of the guns that we have. The enemy has few of these and he takes great care of them. We mainly hit them with Lantsets or tactical ballistic missiles. We will spare nothing for such a dickhead. These French howitzers have taken countless lives of Russian artillerymen.[18]

Using *Lantsets* or ballistic missiles is predicated on the ability of the Russians to detect and direct these relatively slow-flying munitions with long reaction times: no easy task against something as elusive as CAESAR, which may partly explain the low loss rate with only at least four visually confirmed destroyed so far at the time of writing. The weapon has also received some attention in recent Russian publications on the war such as Alyokhin's book on lessons from the 'Special Military Operation', where it is compared to the new Russian *Malva* wheeled SPG (see the previous book in this series on Soviet and Russian SPGs for more details on *Malva*).[19]

While CAESAR was originally designed with an eye to expeditionary operations, its performance in Ukraine has shown that it is a viable weapon in symmetric high-intensity peer warfare. The idea of truck-mounted wheeled artillery systems is also becoming increasingly popular around the world. Some of these have developed into highly advanced systems like the Swedish Archer (used in small numbers by Ukraine);[20] others are much simpler weapons in line with the original CAESAR concept, like the Ukrainian *Bohdana* series (see 'Bohdana' box). Even the Russians, long invested in traditional tracked SPGs, have recently fielded their own analogue to CAESAR in the form of the *Malva*. It is not inconceivable that systems like CAESAR will eventually replace a significant fraction of conventional towed artillery or even heavier tracked SPGs, as it is a relatively inexpensive way of providing artillery pieces with mobility on the modern battlefield while also having a smaller visual and logistical footprint than heavy tracked SPGs.

BOHDANA: MINIMAL CAESAR

Ukraine's first indigenously developed SPG, *Bohdana*'s development history is rather complicated and shrouded in mystery: the first public mentions of the system dating back to at least 2009, when the Ukrainian TASCO Corp. completed development of a then-unnamed prototype wheeled SPG using the KrAZ-6322 6x6 truck chassis and a 155mm howitzer.[21] The name 'Bohdana' was only revealed in July 2018 along with the code 2S22. However, the first pictures of *Bohdana* would not be released until August.[22] *Bohdana* then underwent an extended period of state trials and what could only be described as 'development hell', hampered by incessant disputes between the MOU and *Bohdana*'s primary contractor, KZVV (*Kramatorskyi zavod vazhkogo* verstatobuduvannia, Kramatorsk heavy machinery factory). The pressing needs of the war have accelerated the system's entry into service, with serial production beginning in summer 2022.[23]

Bohdanas on Czech Tatra 158 Phoenix 8x8 chassis February 2024. The resemblance to the French CAESAR concept is pretty apparent. The latest versions feature a semi-automatic loader, whose control panel has been censored in the video this still was taken from. (ZSU General Staff)

There exist multiple variants of *Bohdana* which use the same 155mm L/52 gun mounted on different truck chassis. The original prototype used the KrAZ-63221 6x6 chassis, but the truck's manufacturer, AvtoKrAZ, has historically had significant problems fulfilling defence orders and its bankruptcy in 2021 prohibited it from supplying trucks to the ZSU by law. Thus, later variants of the *Bohdana* have switched to imported Belarusian MAZ-6317 6x6 or Czech Tatra 815-7 and 158 Phoenix 8x8 chassis.[24] All *Bohdana* variants are armed with a 155mm L/52 weapon developed by KZVV compatible with NATO 155mm ammunition. The gun is capable of reaching ~40km using ERFB-BB (extended-range full-bore base bleed) ammunition and up to 60km with RAP. Initially, the gun was loaded entirely manually, but since December 2023 a semi-automatic loader similar in design to the *Pion*'s has been introduced, increasing the rate-of-fire to six rounds/minute. Fire control and aiming of the gun are automatic: like CAESAR, the gun is managed via a control station on the rear left of the vehicle. A panoramic mechanical sight is

Bohdana (Tatra 158 Phoenix) of 45 Art., September 2024 (left). The main control point is visible; as on CAESAR the gun can be aimed automatically by entering coordinates there, though the Ukrainians seem to prefer the gunner (seated next to the gun) doing manual adjustments for better accuracy. (45 Art.)

also provided. A total of 20 rounds are carried onboard in side pannier boxes, as on CAESAR. On all variants, the vehicle cabin is armoured against shrapnel and small arms fire; the latest versions use a cabin made by Ukrayinska Bronetekhnika.[25]

The single *Bohdana* prototype would participate in the bombardment of Russian forces occupying Zmiinyi Island before they withdrew in June 2022, marking the system's first combat use.[26] Production has slowly increased from six SPGs/month in December 2023 to 15–20/month by September 2024, with the assistance of funding from Denmark.[27] It is quite likely that *Bohdana* will become the primary Ukrainian 155mm SPG in the near-future as production continues to increase. A towed variant (popularly called '*Bohdana*-B/BG', although its actual designation is unknown) has also been in development since at least November 2023 and was first unveiled publicly in October 2024: in its current form it is a combination of the *Giatsint*-B carriage with the *Bohdana*'s 155mm ordnance.[28]

Ukrainian analyst Kyrylo Danylchenko once referred to *Bohdana* as '*CAESAR na minimalka*' ('Minimal CAESAR'), while Bohdan Miroshnychenko likened comparing *Bohdana* with CAESAR to comparing a Zaporozhets with a Mercedes.[29] Indeed, the first *Bohdanas* were fairly austere machines, little more than guns on trucks. However, the system has been consistently improved as feedback from the frontlines is taken into account, while still being much cheaper than Western 155mm systems, even the CAESAR. Moreover, regardless of whatever flaws it may have, for the Ukrainians *Bohdana* has the supreme advantage of being made in Ukraine: its supply will not be at the mercy of Western political whims. In fact, the Danish model of providing funding to Ukraine to produce *Bohdanas* with rigorous auditing may be the most sustainable and efficient way for the West to support Ukraine in its war of survival against Russia, if it can be extended to other crucial weapon systems.

7
THE DANA FAMILY: WARSAW PACT TO NATO

Development History

During the Cold War, Czechoslovakia had a relatively advanced industrial base among the non-Soviet Warsaw Pact member states, particularly in the defence sector. It had been a major arms and AFV designer and manufacturer for the Austro-Hungarian Empire and Nazi Germany, and this tradition continued as a part of the Warsaw Pact. Thus, Czechoslovakia could maintain some degree of independence from imported Soviet weapons; in some cases, Czechoslovak products would be adopted by other Warsaw Pact nations or even the USSR itself, as they sometimes proved to be of superior quality to even Soviet manufactured weapons.[1] Sometime in the early 1970s, the state-owned Konštruka Trenčín enterprise was approached by the ČSLA (Czechoslovak People's Army) to develop a 152mm SPG. The ČSLA had been offered the *Akatsiya* by the Soviets, but a domestic product was preferred.[2, 3]

Dana 'Viter' ('Wind') of the 110th 'Gen. Marko Bezruchko' Mechanised Brigade, December 2022. An unknown number of these unmodernised *Danas* were donated by Czechia to Ukraine following the 2022 invasion. (ArmyInform)

At the time, Czechoslovakia did not have a suitable domestic tracked chassis in production, but it did have Tatra: one of the oldest automobile manufacturers still in business and with particular expertise in designing heavy military trucks. They were developing the new Tatra 815 8x8 heavy truck, which demonstrated promising cross-country performance and load-carrying capabilities. Thus, the bold decision was made that the new SPG would be based on the Tatra 815's chassis. The concept of a purpose-built heavy wheeled SPG was unheard of at the time: while armoured cars did exist, no one had ever fielded a 152/155mm howitzer on a wheeled chassis before. The wheeled chassis promised some major benefits (higher road mobility, lower build and running costs, easier maintenance) but required careful design to negate some of the disadvantages (lower cross-country mobility, instability when firing). Another risky decision was to use an autoloader for the 152mm gun, something previously found only on the Swedish 15,5 cm *Bandkanon* 1.

Despite these complexities, the design was completed by 1976 and the nearby ZTS (*Závody ťažkého strojárstva*, Heavy machinery factories) Dubnica nad Váhom was tasked with making it a reality.[4] The prototype was first publicly displayed during a Prague parade in 1980 and the first series-built examples were handed over to the ČSLA the following year as the ShKH vz. 77 *Dana* (*Samohybná kanónová húfnica vzor* 77 dělo automobilní nabíjené automaticky, Self-propelled gun-howitzer model [19]77 on automotive [chassis] loaded automatically), often shortened to simply '*Dana*'.[5] *Dana* would also be adopted by Poland, though most other Warsaw Pact nations opted for the *Akatsiya*. Some were even purchased by the Soviets, where they ended up in Georgia after the USSR's break-up and were used during the 2008 Russian invasion.[6]

Dana development continued throughout the 1980s. Much like the Soviets with the *Akatsiya*, the Czechoslovaks were not satisfied with the *Dana*'s 152mm L/37 howitzer's insufficient range. This led to the *Ondava* modernisation project, which primarily sought to increase range by switching to a 152mm L/47 barrel. However, the end of the Cold War in 1992 saw the mutually peaceful break-up of Czechoslovakia into independent Czechia and Slovakia as well as significant cutbacks in defence spending in both nations. Thus, *Ondava* would not enter service with either the new Czech or Slovak armies.[7] Still, the work would not go to waste, for now that they were no longer beholden to the Warsaw Pact standard 152mm calibre and with an eye towards NATO and the international export market, Konštruka Trenčín would base the new 155mm *Zuzana* SPG on *Ondava*. Armed with a domestic 155mm L/45 barrel, the original *Zuzana* would only end up being adopted in relatively small numbers by Slovakia and Greece, despite attempts to market it abroad.[8]

Today the *Dana* family has diverged into two distinct development branches, one Slovak and the other Czech, with many different variants offered for sale. For brevity, only the ones used by Ukraine will be described in this section. In addition to the original *Dana*, they are:[9, 10]

- *Zuzana* 2: redesign of the *Zuzana* with a JBMoU-compatible 155mm L/52, offered by Slovakia's DMD Group (which includes both Konštruka-Defence and ZTS-Špeciál, the renamed designer and manufacturer of the *Dana*).
- *Dana* M2: modernisation of the original *Dana* that retains the 152mm howitzer, produced by the Czech company Excalibur Army in Šternberk.
- *Dita*: private initiative by Excalibur Army, essentially *Dana* M2 with the original *Zuzana*'s 155mm L/45 instead of the 152mm L/37 and a new turret.

The technical summary will focus on the original *Dana* as its basis, but will note known significant differences introduced on the *Zuzana* 2, *Dana* M2, and *Dita*.

Technical Summary

The *Dana* and *Dana* M2 are armed with a 152mm L/37 howitzer developed domestically in Czechoslovakia. It is capable of accepting the Soviet OF-540 (manufactured in Czechoslovakia as 152-EOF-KH-37), which can be fired at ~690m/s out to 18.7km.[11, 12] Extended-range ammunition has also been developed by Czechia and Slovakia for the *Dana*, including hollow-base (20km) and BB (25.5km) shells. *Zuzana* 2 is armed with a JBMoU-compliant 155mm L/52 weapon, and is thus capable of accepting any NATO standard 155mm ammunition and has a significantly longer range than the 152mm L/37. In both cases, a horizontal sliding-breech block is used; however, since NATO 155mm charges do not come in metal cases like Soviet 152mm charges, the *Zuzana* 2's breech also has been modified with an obturator. *Dita*'s 155mm L/45 weapon is

Zuzana 2 of an unknown Ukrainian unit in Kurakhove, February 2023. *Zuzana* 2 is most easily recognised by the new armoured front cab and the double-baffle muzzle brake on the 155mm L/52. Footage of the system in Ukrainian service has been quite limited. (GuerrillaMedicine.eu)

Dana M2 of the 56th 'Mariupol' Motorised Brigade, fall 2024. *Dana* M2 has a redesigned front cab with large bulletproof windows for better visibility and a modern FCS, but retains the old 152mm howitzer and turret with some modifications. (ArmyTV)

Dana 'Manyunya' of 110 Mech. firing at Russian positions, Avdiivka front, February 2024. No fume extractor is used since the crew are protected from gun fumes in the enclosed turret and cab compartments. (110 Mech.)

also compatible with NATO 155mm rounds, though L/45 is not standardised within NATO. It is capable of reaching 39km with BB shells.

The main gun is mounted within an angular turret located in the middle of the vehicle and fed by an autoloader in the exposed central trough of the turret. The autoloader consists of the shell transfer arm, charge transfer arm, hydraulic chain rammer, and two conveyor magazine racks. It is capable of loading the gun at any elevation angle without human intervention. On *Dana* and *Dana M2*, 36 projectiles and charges each are stored vertically within these magazines, with up to 24 more in stowage racks in the turret and hull: the latter must be retrieved manually. *Zuzana* 2 and *Dita* carry 40 rounds each, all stowed within the conveyor magazines. Their autoloaders have also been redesigned to handle NATO modular charges, but not bagged charges: these can only be used with manual loading. The maximum rate-of-fire is five rounds/minute (six for *Dita*) with the autoloader. In *Dana*/*Dana M2*, one loader sits behind the projectile magazine in a separate compartment on the turret's right side, responsible for overseeing the autoloader's functionality. The gunner and a second loader (responsible for restocking the charge magazine) are seated in front of the charge magazine on the turret's left side. *Dita* has a redesigned turret with windows on the left of the turret for a gunner, who is only there if manual aiming is needed.

The original *Dana* has traditional manual fire controls, relying on the ZZ-73 mechanical sight with adapted Soviet PG-1M-D indirect fire panoramic telescope, OP-5-38D direct-fire telescopic sight, and PAB-2A artillery compass, and thus requires artillery surveys before firing. The modernised *Dana M2*, *Dita*, and *Zuzana* 2 have automated gun-laying systems with integrated INS/SNS. *Dana M2* still retains the ZZ-73 as the ZZ-73 M64, converted to NATO standards.[13] *Zuzana* 2 has a TV and thermal camera as well as a laser rangefinder for direct fire, plus a PAZ-2001 aiming device with PP-81MN panoramic telescope as a manual backup for both direct and indirect fire. It is not publicly known what *Dita* uses as a manual backup. On *Dana*/*Dana M2*, the turret allows for +/-225° traverse (full 360° for *Zuzana* 2; possibly the same for *Dita*) and can elevate the gun up to 70° (75° for *Zuzana* 2), although firing is restricted to +/-45° (60° for *Zuzana* 2 and *Dita*) off-axis at elevations above 10°. Three extendable hydraulic stabiliser supports are provided for added stability: two under the turret on each side of the vehicle and one under the engine in the rear.

The crew and ammunition are protected by armour plating whose thicknesses are not publicly known. *Zuzana* 2 is rated at STANAG 4569 Level 3 ballistic protection and Level 1 mine protection; it is reasonable to assume that the protection level is similar on *Dana*/*Dana M2* and *Dita*. The crew compartments are NBC-protected and air-conditioned. *Dana M2* and *Zuzana* 2 also have smoke grenade launchers on the turret face. All variants also have an AAMG mounted on the first loader's hatch on the turret's right side: on the original *Dana*, it is a 12.7mm PLK vz. 38/46 (Czechoslovak DShK); on *Dana M2*, a 12.7mm *Utyos* (NSVT); on *Zuzana* 2, a .50 Browning M2 is used instead.

Dana and *Dana M2* have a crew of five: the driver and commander sit in the front armoured cab, with the gunner and two loaders in the turret. *Zuzana* 2 has a four-person crew: its armoured cab only seats the driver, with the commander moved to the former second loader's position. *Dita* can seat three but requires a crew of only two: the driver and commander in the front cab. *Dita*'s turret can be operated from the cab using the M4 control panel of the Onboard Control System. Emplacement/displacement times are not given for *Dana*/*Dana M2* or *Zuzana* 2 in promotional material; however, a video by Excalibur Army demonstrated that *Dita* is capable of opening fire within about 32 seconds of halting, conducting three-round MRSI at 13km range within one minute, and displacing in 28 seconds, for a total fire mission time of two minutes and five seconds.[14]

As noted before, the *Dana*/*Zuzana* chassis is derived from the Tatra 815 truck in its 8x8 form, lengthened and reversed with the engine in the rear. The specific armoured chassis used by the original

Dana autoloader being demonstrated as viewed from behind (top) and above (bottom). The shell transfer arm takes shells from the conveyor magazine in the turret's right side, and moves them into position to be rammed in by the chain rammer. The process is then repeated for charges from the turret's left side using the charge transfer arm. Visible at the bottom of the trough is the conveyor belt used to remove spent cases from the turret; *Zuzana* 2 and *Dita* use NATO charges without metal cases and thus dispense with this feature. (110 Mech.)

A Czech BVP-2 (Czechoslovak-built BMP-2) IFV being loaded onto a Tatra 815 truck. The Tatra 815's excellent load-carrying capacity and cross-country performance thanks to the Tatra suspension design made it a natural choice to base the *Dana* (bottom) and its derivatives on. Each suspension unit has air bellows, allowing for ground clearance to be adjusted as seen here with the first two front axles. (Łukasz Golowanow; 110 Mech.)

Dana has the designation 'Tatra 815 VP 31 29 275 8x8.1R'; it is not publicly known for the other SPGs. Tatra trucks rely on the so-called 'Tatra concept' pioneered by the company in the 1920s as the secret to their outstanding cross-country mobility: this involves the use of a central load-carrying tube and axles with independently suspended swinging half-axles bolted together into a single unit. Each unit has leaf springs, telescopic shock absorbers, and air bellows. All axles are driven by Tatra's unique differential design with two opposing spiral bevel gears instead of just one; the two front axles can be steered.[15]

The original 29.3t *Dana* is powered by a 360hp Tatra 3-930-52M V-12 turbocharged air-cooled 4-stroke diesel engine paired with a Tatra 10+2-speed gearbox providing a power/weight ratio of ~12hp/t. The 30.2t *Dana* M2 uses the modernised Tatra 3-930.52M providing the same power but switches to a Tatra-Norgren 10 TS 130 10+2-speed semi-automatic gearbox. *Dita* uses a chassis with a front cab similar in design to the *Dana* M2, but is lighter at 29t. It has a 409hp Tatra T3C-928-90 V-8 diesel engine. *Zuzana* 2 is considerably heavier at 33.8t and has a more powerful 435hp Tatra 3B-928.70 V-8 diesel engine paired with a Tatra 14 TS 210L-N 14+2-speed synchromesh gearbox.[16] *Dana* M2, *Dita*, and *Zuzana* 2 have advertised top road speeds of 90km/h and also feature APUs for operating with the extended operations with the engine switched off.

Context

Ukrainian interest in the *Dana* family predates the 2022 invasion, with an order for 26 *Dana* M2s being placed as early as 2020 with Excalibur Army.[17] Following the invasion, an unknown number of original *Danas* have been donated by Czechia to Ukraine; interestingly, Poland is not known to have sent theirs at the time of writing, even though they are transitioning fully towards the 155mm calibre. Slovakia has donated eight *Zuzana* 2s, with a further 16 ordered by Ukraine and funded by Denmark, Germany, and Norway. The shorter-ranged *Dana* and *Dana* M2 appear to have been distributed to Ukrainian mechanised and motorised brigades such as the 110th Mechanised Brigade, taking the place of the *Akatsiya*; it is not publicly known yet which units operate the *Zuzana* 2.

Dana 'Slavutych' of 110 Mech. on the move. Wheeled vehicles are far faster than most tracked vehicles on roads, giving them much greater strategic mobility if a decent road network is available. (110 Mech.)

Given that *Dana* was originally designed as a Czechoslovak alternative to the *Akatsiya*, it is perhaps best to have a former *Akatsiya* commander, 'Yuriy' of 110 Mech., give his commentary on the *Dana*:

The Dana SPGs are similar to the Soviet *Akatsiya*, but there are also very significant differences. The most important difference that makes Dana highly mobile is the Tatra wheeled platform. It allows you to move quickly on the highway, and the tracked *Akatsiya* loses to it in this. In addition, the track life is very limited, so in modern warfare, when high mobility is required, this is also a definite problem. Another difference is the open gun mounting, so when fired, gun fumes do not get inside and the crew is not affected. But I think the most important thing is that ammunition is loaded in automatic mode. This allows you to increase the rate of fire and reduce the time spent in the firing position. Despite its venerable age (the gun was manufactured in 1984), all mechanisms work well, and given the characteristics of the machine, we are definitely a desirable target for the enemy.[18]

It is worth noting that the *Dana* M2 and *Zuzana* 2 have automated fire control, which gives them a greater advantage in terms of responsiveness compared to *Dana* and *Akatsiya*.

Zuzana 2 is a highly capable and modern system on paper but, unfortunately, appears to have suffered serious reliability problems ranging from hydraulic system failures to wear and deformation of the breech block and the trigger mechanism, as well as engine failures. In some cases, the SPG failed after a few days of operations. Whether this is a design flaw or operator error is uncertain.[19] Deliveries and repairs of the system have also been slow: only two of the 16 SPGs ordered in October 2022 have been delivered at the time of writing, and of the eight *Zuzana* 2s sent back to Slovakia for repair, only two had returned to service by July 2024. Presumably this is why very little footage of the *Zuzana* 2 has been published in Ukrainian service. The Slovakian Fico government elected in 2023 is relatively hostile towards Ukraine, thus the future of the system in Ukrainian service is rather questionable. *Dana* M2 seems to have fared better in terms of reliability, and is described by 'Ruslan' of the 56th Mariupol Motorised Brigade as 'very, very effective' and who also praised its high accuracy (dispersion of the first shot <50 m), mobility, and ease of use.[20] *Dita* has only recently arrived in Ukraine, though initial feedback from the NHU's Azov Brigade appears to be quite positive. 'Vorzel', a *Dita* commander in the brigade, was particularly complimentary of the system's automation and quick reaction times.[21]

Dana was a very radical design for the 1970s, with the only other contemporary wheeled SPG being the South African G6; while its 152mm L/37 did not have the long-range provided by the G6's 155mm L/45, the *Dana* also incorporated a fully automatic loading system. This may be the reason why *Dana* and its descendants have not experienced much success on the export market, as militaries tend to be fairly conservative institutions. However, that may be changing; the French CAESAR, while a less sophisticated system, has shown that there is a market for wheeled SPGs, and its use in Ukraine along with the *Dana* family have proved beyond doubt that they are as capable as their tracked counterparts as artillery weapons, while also offering higher strategic mobility given a reasonable road network. Other manufacturers like Germany and the ROK are also developing wheeled SPGs, with notably the former's Boxer RCH 155 set to enter Ukrainian service sometime in the near future.[22] Perhaps the future will be brighter for the *Dana*'s various descendants being offered by both Czechia and Slovakia.

Dita of the NHU's Azov Brigade, December 2024. *Ditas* have only recently arrived in Ukraine, but have so far been received positively by their users. (Azov)

ARCHER: SWEDISH UNICORN

As a part of its 'total defence' strategy, Sweden maintains respectable domestic defence industrial capabilities, including artillery production under the famous Bofors company (today part of BAE). During the Cold War, Sweden developed its own 155mm artillery pieces: the *Bandkanon* 1 (lit. 'tracked gun') SPG and *Fälthaubits* 77 (FH 77) towed field howitzer. Both designs emphasised a high burst rate-of-fire and a high degree of automation. When it entered service in 1967, the *Bandkanon* was the world's first 155mm SPG with an autoloader; its 15,5cm kan m/60 L/50 gun could fire the entire 15-round load in 45 seconds out to 25km. However, it was also very heavy (53t) and underpowered (240/300hp), restricting the top speed to 28km/h.[23] The L/38 FH 77A, which entered service in 1978, featured a hydraulic rammer, allowing it to fire three rounds in eight seconds out to 21km during burst-firing. It was also the world's first towed 155mm gun with an APU for limited autonomous movement and to speed up emplacement/displacement.[24] Both used their own unique fixed and semi-fixed 155mm ammunition, and were thus completely incompatible with NATO 155mm ammunition.

Bofors thus developed the L/39 FH 77B to use NATO ammunition for the export market. This variant was sold to India and Nigeria, but became embroiled in a huge scandal

Heavily camouflaged Archer 6x6 SPG of 45 Art. somewhere in Donetsk *oblast*, January 2024. The large armoured housing behind the gun contains the projectile and charge magazines, stored as far away from the crew as possible for their safety. The remote weapon station is not fitted.

when it was revealed that Bofors had paid the equivalent of $2.4 billion (2023 value) in bribes to Swedish and Indian officials to secure the contract, the largest arms sale in Swedish history.[25] As a result of the so-called 'Bofors scandal', India did not end up exercising an option to buy a second batch of FH 77Bs, which Bofors had already produced 50 of, thus the Swedish government bailed Bofors out by forcing the Swedish Army to buy them instead in 1990.[26] By this time, the Swedish MoD had begun looking into requirements for a new SPG to replace the ageing *Bandkanon* under the APS 2000 (*Artilleripjäs splitterskyddad*, protected artillery piece) project. To reduce development and life cycle costs, the Volvo A30 6x6 articulated dump truck was ultimately chosen as the platform for what was known as 'REMO (*renovering och modifiering*, renovation and modification) *av Haubits 77*', i.e. a modernisation programme for existing FH 77 howitzers.[27] The first prototypes were based around an L/45 version of the FH 77A on A30D (FH 77AD), but soon switched to the FH 77B on A30E (FH 77BD). Bofors had also developed an L/52 version of the FH 77B, which was integrated with the system in 2006.[28]

The first examples were delivered to the Swedish Army in 2015 as the *Artillerisystem* 08 Archer.[29] Strictly speaking, the Archer system consists of two vehicles: the SPG based on the Volvo A30E 6x6 articulated truck (known as 'Archer Mobile Howitzer 6x6' in the BAE brochure), as well as the *Ammunitionshanteringssystemet* (AMH, ammunition handling system) resupply module in a modified standard ISO container that can be mounted on standard cargo trucks. The latter carries 100 rounds and can resupply an Archer in five minutes.[30] Besides the 6x6 A30E, BAE also offers the Archer SPG on 8x8 or 10x10 platforms. Until 2023, Sweden would be the only user of the Archer, with 48 systems built. Denmark and Norway were at various points participants in the project, but both had withdrawn before its completion. In March 2023, the Swedish government announced that it would donate eight Archers to Ukraine, which were subsequently delivered by November that year.[31] Simultaneously, the UK, having donated a significant fraction of its AS90s to Ukraine as well, has also bought 14 Archers from Sweden as a temporary replacement pending the arrival of the Boxer RCH 155.[32]

The Archer's FH 77BW L/52 gun is compatible with NATO standard 155mm ammunition and uses modular charges. It is placed in a telescoping breech mount, allowing it to be retracted into the magazine when stowed to fit behind the crew cabin within a protective casing. It is fed by an autoloader with a burst rate-of-fire of three rounds in 20 seconds, or all 21 rounds in three minutes. The magazine is contained within a splinter-proof armoured housing behind the gun with a capacity for 21 shells, 126 modular charges (maximum six per shell), and 40 primer cartridges. The entire gun assembly can be elevated up to 70° and traversed 85° left/right. The 34t vehicle is powered by a 343hp Volvo D9B AC E3 diesel engine, allowing for a top road speed of 70km/h.[33] The crew sits in an armoured cabin in front of the vehicle and, unlike on CAESAR, they can conduct an entire fire mission without leaving its protection, other than to restock ammunition in the magazines. While the nominal crew consists of four people (compared to 10 for an FH 77), it is possible for a single person to operate the SPG. The cabin also has an optional remote weapon station on top armed with a .50 Browning M2 heavy MG. As with all modern Western artillery systems, the Archer is equipped with a sophisticated fire control, navigation, and communications suite, and it is capable of emplacing and opening fire or displacing within 20 seconds.[34]

The only Ukrainian unit known to use the Archer is the 45th Artillery Brigade, where it serves alongside the *Bohdana* and towed guns. There has been very little public information about the Archer's service in Ukraine, although it was briefly featured in a 2024 United24 video. They spoke to 'Yurii', who had two years of experience as an artilleryman on 152mm D-20 towed howitzers before transferring to the Archer after a two-month crash training course: 'Before our training trip, my friend told me this was the best thing in artillery that was ever invented. And now, I realise he was right…I believe that the Archer is a sniper howitzer. It hits straight on target, not aiming in squares, but directly into it. Literally in 1–2 shots.'[35]

The Archer represents a more sophisticated solution to providing mobility to towed artillery, with greater automation and protection than CAESAR provides, while still being considerably cheaper than modern tracked SPGs such as the PzH 2000 to both procure and maintain. It was claimed in a 2005 Swedish MoD proposal that the Archer would cost five times less than the PzH 2000 to operate, while still allowing an artillery company of six pieces to reduce its operating personnel from 150 (FH 77B) to 50 thanks to its automation.[36] If this is correct, Archer may be an attractive option for the Ukrainians as a higher-end supplement to CAESAR and *Bohdana*, but at the time of writing there is no evidence that they intend to buy more Archers.

APPENDIX: PROJECTILES

The following are lists of projectiles for the various artillery calibres described in the book. These lists are not comprehensive and are mostly restricted to HE, cluster, and guided munitions used for indirect fire missions. They do not include munitions such as direct-fire anti-tank, smoke, leaflet, illumination, electronic countermeasures etc.

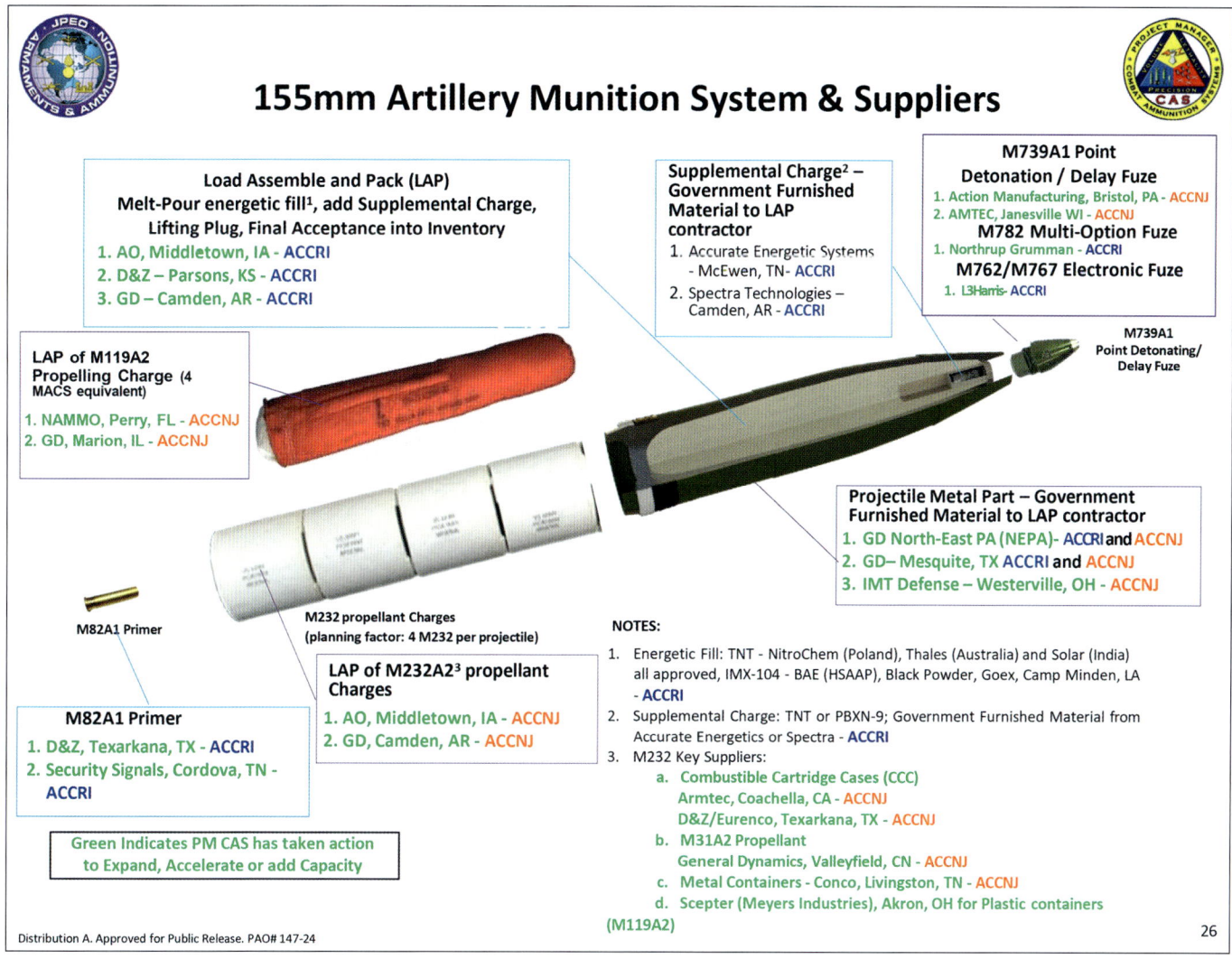

Cutaway of a 155mm round consisting of the M795 HE projectile, M739A1 fuse, and M232A2 modular charges or M119A2 bagged charge, as well as manufacturers of their components. M795 is the standard 155mm HE projectile used by the US military. M739A1 is a point-detonating fuse, i.e. it explodes the round immediately upon or shortly after impact. (DTIC)

Weight of projectile includes the fuse unless otherwise noted, and may vary between individual shells depending on filling and manufacturing batch, thus should only be taken as a rough guide.

Shell lethality is a complex matter depending on many factors other than the explosive content and type, including angle of fall, projectile shape, and casing thickness, all of which can affect the fragmentation pattern. The filler content is provided only to give some idea of their relative effectiveness.

105mm

Only American 105mm M1 type ammunition is used by 105mm artillery currently serving in Ukraine. They are not interchangeable with British 105mm Fd ammunition as used on British L118 Light Guns. Semi-fixed ammunition with brass charge cases.

Name	Weight (kg)	Filler / Payload	Notes
HE M1	16	2.3kg Comp B (normal cavity)	US HE shell. TNT filler may also be used.
HERA M927	17.9	2.6kg TNT	US HE RAP. 19km max range.
HE PFF-BB M1130	16.3	PBX4 + tungsten spheres	US HE BB shell with pre-formed fragments. 13.5km max range.

155mm

Ammunition is separate-loading using either bagged or modular charges. Most 155mm ammunition can be used by any JBMoU-compliant gun. However, shells from different countries can vary significantly in terms of their ballistic properties and handling. This is further complicated by the various charge types used by Ukrainian forces. Maximum range of shells fitted with BB tail: 30km (L/39), 39–40km (L/52).

Name	Weight (kg)	Filler / Payload	Notes
HE M107	43.2	6.8kg TNT	Second World War US HE shell used only for training in Western militaries, but often used as a combat round in Ukraine and elsewhere. Manufactured in many other countries.
HE M795	46.9	10.8kg TNT	Standard US HE shell, replacing M107.
M712 Copperhead	62.4	6.7kg Comp. B	US laser-guided HEAT shell with guidance fins. 16km maximum range from L/39.
M718A1/M741A1 RAAMS	47	9 x AT mines	Remote Anti-Armor Mine System. US long (48h)/short (4h) duration AT mine-dispersal shells. Each mine contains 0.6kg PBX-0280 explosive. 17.5km max range.
M692/M731 ADAM	47	9 x anti-personnel mines	Area Denial Artillery Munitions. US long (48h)/short (4h) duration anti-personnel mine-dispersal shells. Each mine contains 0.6kg PBX-0280 explosive. 17.5km max range.
HERA M549/ M549A1	43.5	7.3kg Comp. B/6.8kg TNT	US HE RAP. 30km max range with M203, 23.5km otherwise. M549 cannot be fired with M203.
HE M483A1	46.5	88 x DPICM	US cluster munitions shell. 64 x M42 (0.035kg Comp. A4) and 24 x M46 (2.8kg Comp. A5) HEAT-fragmentation DPICM. 17.7km max range.
DP M864	47	72 x DPICM	US extended-range BB cluster munitions shell. 48 x M42 (0.035kg Comp. A4) and 24 x M46 (2.8kg Comp. A5) HEAT-fragmentation DPICM. 28km max range with M203.
M982A1 Excalibur	48	5.4kg PBXN-9	US-Swedish GPS/INS-guided HE RAP. Max range: 40km (L/39), 50km (L/52).
L15/L15A1	43.5	11.1/11.3kg Comp. B	British thin-walled hollow-base HE shell.
DM121	43.5	10.6kg Comp. B / PBX RH 26	German thin-walled HE shell. Comes in hollow-base or BB variants. Also produced in Spain as ER02A1.
DM702 SMArt 155	47.3	2 x EFP submunition	SMArt (*Suchzündermunition Artillerie*, artillery sensor-fused munition). German anti-armour sensor-fused munition. Each parachute-retarded submunition has 4.2kg EFP warhead with IR + millimetric radar sensors. Max range: 22km (L/39), 27km (L/52).
KTA 5938/5934	43	9kg HE	Finnish thin-walled HE shell. Differ in terms of driving bands.
OFd MKM	43.6	10kg TNT	Slovak HE shell. Comes in hollow-base or BB variants.
LU 211	43.3	8.8kg TNT / Comp. B / EIDS XF 13 333	Modern French HE shell. Comes in hollow-base or BB variants. Insensitive munitions-compliant.
OE 155 F1	42.2	8.8kg TNT / Comp. B	1990s French HE shell. Comes in hollow-base or BB variants.
BONUS	44.6	2 x AC F1 BON	BONUS — Bofors Nutating Shell. Franco-Swedish anti-armour sensor-fused munition with BB. Each submunition has 6.5kg EFP warhead with IR + lidar sensors. Max range: 27km (L/39), 35km (L/52).
EFRB BB/BT	47.5	~8.7kg TNT	Long HE shell with 4 stabilising bourrelet nubs. Shells of this type are manufactured in Slovakia, India, Pakistan, and South Africa under different names.

SELECTED BIBLIOGRAPHY

Military Manuals/Textbooks/Manufacturer Brochures
All material in English unless otherwise noted. The ZSU also publishes 'methodical guides' (*metodichnyi posibnyk*) in Ukrainian for some of its Western weapon systems.

L119/M119
BAE Systems, '*105mm Light Gun*' brochure (2016)

M777
ST-3-09.71: M777A2 Lightweight 155mm Howitzer (LW155) Tactics, Techniques and Procedures (TTP) (Draft, 2009)
BAE Systems, '*155mm Lightweight Field Howitzer M777*' brochure (2022)

M109
TM 9-2350-311-10: Operator's Manual for Howitzer, Medium, Self-Propelled, 155mm M109A2, M109A3, M109A4, M109A5 (1994)
TM 9-2350-314-10: Operator's Manual for Howitzer, Medium, Self-Propelled, 155mm M109A6 (1999)
FM 3-09.70: Tactics, Techniques, and Procedures for M109A6 Howitzer (Paladin) Operations (2000)
SVP 7-(07)256: *Metodichnyi posibnyk* "155-mm *samokhidna haubytsia* M109A3GN, M109A4" (2023) [Ukrainian]
Flanders Technical Supply (FTS), '*M109A4 BE 155mm self-propelled medium howitzer*' brochure

Panzerhaubitze 2000
KMW, '*PzH 2000 — The Euro Howitzer*' brochure (2003)

AS90
Horstman, 'Hydrogas' brochure (2024)

Krab
HSW, '*155 mm samobieżna haubica na podwoziu gąsienicowym Krab*' brochure (2021)

CAESAR
SVP 7-(07)268: *Metodichnyi posibnyk* "155-mm *samokhidna haubytsia* CAESAR" (2023) [Ukrainian]
Nexter, '*CAESAR 6x6*' brochure (2018)
Renault Trucks Defense, '*Sherpa 5 Euro 4 Long Cab Wheelbase 4500 mm*' brochure (2006).

Dana & Zuzana
Excalibur Army, '*Artillery Systems*' catalogue
KONŠTRUKTA – Defence, *Zuzana* 2 leaflets (2017 & 2021)
Tatra Trucks, '*Performance & Data Sheets: Tatra Military Vehicles*'

Misc.
TM 43-0001-28: Army Ammunition Data Sheets (2003)
US Army Defense Ammunition Center, '*Hazard Classification of United States Military Explosives and Munitions*' (2012)

Books
Dastrup, B., *King of Battle: A Branch History of the US Army's Field Artillery* (TRADOC, 1991)
Hunnicutt, R., *Sheridan: A History of the American Light Tank, Vol. 2* (Presidio, 2023)
Schneider, W., *Panzerhaubitze 2000: Entwicklung—Technik—Einsatz* (Motorbuch Verlag, 2023) [German]
Korán, F., & Horák, J., *DANA ShKH vz.77 in detail* (WWP, 2011)
Spurný, J., *AS-90 Braveheart in detail* (WWP, 2003)
Manson, M., *Guns, Mortars and Rockets* (Brassey's, 1997)
Geneva International Centre for Humanitarian Demining, 'Explosive Ordnance Guide for Ukraine' (2022)

Periodicals
Janes' International Defence Review (IDR)
Janes' Defence Weekly (JDW)
Nowa Tekhnika Wojskowa (NTW) [Polish]

Online Resources
British Artillery of World War 2 (britishartillery.co.uk, also at nigelef.tripod.com): extensive resource by Nigel Evans on artillery technique and technology from a British perspective, mostly covering the Second World War, but also the Cold War and beyond.
Ammunition 155 mm (en.bk155.com.ua) [English/Ukrainian]: Oleh Sirota's Ukrainian website on 155mm ammunition and operating the various 155mm systems in service.
Valka.cz (valka.cz) [English/Czech]: Czech website that covers weapons from around the world, but particularly detailed for Czechoslovak, Czech, and Slovak weapons.

ENDNOTES

Introduction

1. 'Soldiers: A History of Men in Battle – Gunner', BBC (1985).

Chapter 1

1. S. Bidwell, *Artillery Tactics 1939–1945* (1976), p.21.
2. S. Moberg, '*Supporting 'Our Boys': How The Royal Artillery Became A WWII Battle-Winner*', Forces News (2018): forcesnews.com/services/army/supporting-our-boys-how-royal-artillery-became-wwii-battle-winner
3. B. Dastrup, *King of Battle* (1991), p.259.
4. Dastrup, pp.268–270.
5. European Defence Agency, '*Expert Group 10 Ammunition Final Report*' (2021), p.9.
6. Rheinmetall Nitrochemie, '*155mm Artillery Modular Charge System*' (brochure), p.2.
7. RBC-Ukraine, '*Polkovnik Serhiy Musienko: My izmenili taktiku primeneniya artillerii v voyne*' (2024): rbc.ua/ukr/news/polkovnik-sergiy-musienko-mi-otrimuemo-vdvichi-1731872952.html

Chapter 2

1. N. Evans, '*Artillery Methods*' (2016): nigelef.tripod.com/maindoc.htm
2. N. Evans, '*25-pdr*' (2014): nigelef.tripod.com/25pdrsheet.htm
3. Garrington gun exhibit placard at Royal Artillery Museum: flickr.com/photos/sarge_schultz/1673317042/in/photostream/
4. N. Evans, '*25-pdr*' (2014): nigelef.tripod.com/25pdrsheet.htm
5. O. Díez, '*Artillery and Missiles*' (2000), pp.10–15.
6. N. Evans, '*The 105 mm Light Gun*' (2015): nigelef.tripod.com/p_105ltgun.htm
7. Díez, '*Artillery and Missiles*', pp.4–9.
8. DoD, '*Fiscal Year (FY) 2024 Budget Estimates: Army, Justification Book Vol. 1 of 1*' (2023), pp.202–217.
9. D. Gallagher, '*Top Guns*', Army Magazine (Aug 1989), pp.27–29.
10. Militarnyi, '*Ukraine received 105mm M927 high-explosive rocket-assisted projectiles*' (2022): mil.in.ua/en/news/ukraine-received-105mm-m927-high-explosive-rocket-assisted-projectiles/
11. Rbl.F. — *Rundblickfehrnrohr* ('panoramic sight').
12. Hall & Watts Defence Optics Ltd., '*Artillery Sighting System*': hallandwatts.com/products/artillery-sighting-system/
13. G. Legler, '*160th Field Artillery live fire new artillery systems*', DVIDS (2018): dvidshub.net/news/294685/160th-field-artillery-live-fire-new-artillery-systems
14. MOD, '*UK to send scores of artillery guns and hundreds of drones to Ukraine*' (2022): gov.uk/government/news/uk-to-send-scores-of-artillery-guns-and-hundreds-of-drones-to-ukraine
15. New Zealand Defence Force, '*NZDF Artillery Team to Train Ukrainians alongside UK*' (2022): nzdf.mil.nz/media-centre/news/nzdf-artillery-team-to-train-ukrainians-alongside-uk/
16. Defense Express, '*British L119 105mm Howitzer is Already in Ukraine: Military Told About its Advantages Over the Soviet D-30*' (2022): en.defence-ua.com/weapon_and_tech/british_l119_105mm_howitzer_is_already_in_ukraine_military_told_about_its_advantages_over_the_soviet_d_30-3785.html
17. ArmyTV, '*THE BRITISH L118 HOWITZER DESTROYS RUSSIAN TROOPS: AFU defeats Russian invaders with Western aid*' (2024): youtu.be/iXRfAgXmugM
18. V. Nazarkevich and O. Vikarchuk, '*Okupanty zayshly v garazh i zakryly dveri. V tsyu myt my nakryly iyogo vognem — komandyr harmaty M119 pro robotu rozrahunku*', ArmyInform (2023): armyinform.com.ua/2023/05/28/okupanty-zajshly-v-garazh-i-zakryly-dveri-v-czyu-myt-my-nakryly-jogo-vognem-komandyr-garmaty-m119-pro-robotu-rozrahunku/
19. (Pinned comment) Ukrainian Soldier Channel, '*British L119 Light Howitzer - Queen of Light Artillery*', YouTube (2023): youtu.be/SttJguD7P5A
20. Ukrainian Ministry of Strategic Industries, '*Mizhnarodnyy oboronnyy vyrobnyk BAE SYSTEMS vidkryvaye ofis v Ukrayini dlya realizatsiyi spilnykh proektiv z vyrobnytstva zbroyi*' (2023): mspu.gov.ua/news/mizhnarodnyi-oboronnyi-vyrobnyk-bae-systems-vidkryvaie-ofis-v-ukraini-dlia-realizatsii-spilnykh-proektiv-z-vyrobnytstva-zbroi
21. R. Pengelley, '*155mm firepower for less than 4t: VSEL's Ultra-lightweight Field Howitzer*', IDR Vol. 22, Issue 11 (1989), pp.1533–1540.
22. P. Clark, '*The XM777 Joint Lightweight 155mm Howitzer Program (LW155): A Case Study in Program Management Considerations Concerning the Use of National Arsenal Assets*' (2003), pp.8–16.
23. Canadian M777C1s use the British Laser Inertial Artillery Pointing System (LINAPS) also found on British L118s. This appears to have been retained on M777C1s sent to Ukraine.
24. IDR 11/1989 reports a direct-fire telescope taken from 106mm M40 recoilless rifles can be fitted, but this has not been seen in Ukraine.
25. FUNKER530, '*Ukrainian Artillery Team Takes M777 Out Of Action In Expert Time*', YouTube (2022): youtu.be/kRdQKpdMIZQ
26. Pengelley, '*Ultra-lightweight Field Howitzer*', pp.1533–1540.
27. US Army Acquisition Support Center, '*It's All In The Deliv-ery*' (2023): asc.army.mil/web/news-its-all-in-the-deliv-ery/
28. C. Jacobs, '*Wild Video Shows Ford Super Duty Pickup Towing an M777 Howitzer in Ukraine*', The Drive (2023): thedrive.com/news/you-can-tow-an-m777-howitzer-with-a-ford-super-duty-if-you-need-to
29. United24, '*M777 Howitzer on the Frontline. Watch Ukrainian artillery fire on Russian positions near Bakhmut*', YouTube (2023): youtu.be/hampti9aXmE
30. BAE Systems, '*New contract presents optimum conditions for a likely restart of M777 production*' (2024): baesystems.com/en/article/us-army-signs-agreement-with-bae-systems-for-new-m777-structures
31. RBC-Ukraine, '*Polkovnik Serhiy Musienko*'.
32. A. Roque, '*Towed artillery has reached 'end of the effectiveness,' Army four-star declares*', Breaking Defense (2024): breakingdefense.com/2024/03/towed-artillery-has-reached-end-of-the-effectiveness-army-four-star-declares/
33. M. Zabrodskyi, J. Watling, O. Danylyuk, and N. Reynolds, '*Preliminary Lessons in Conventional Warfighting from Russia's Invasion of Ukraine: February–July 2022*', RUSI (2022) pp.38–39.
34. RBC-Ukraine, '*Polkovnik Serhiy Musienko*'.

Chapter 3

1. R. Hunnicutt, '*Sheridan: A History of the American Light Tank, Vol. 2*' (1995), pp.205–209.
2. Dastrup, *King of Battle*, pp.259–260.
3. Hunnicutt, '*Sheridan*', p.213.
4. Hunnicutt, '*Sheridan*', pp.216–220.
5. FTS M109A4 BE brochure.
6. Army Guide, '*M109L*': army-guide.com/eng/product3729.html
7. Doppeladler, '*Panzerhaubitze M109 A5Ö*': doppeladler.com/oebh/artillerie/m109a5.htm
8. TM 9-2300-216-10 C6, pp.3-120–3-121.
9. FTS M109A4 BE brochure.
10. Doppeladler, '*M109 A5Ö*'.
11. The author has been told by his NHU acquaintance that in their unit the M109Ls have been modified to use Soviet PG-1 panoramic periscopes.
12. Doppeladler, '*M109 A5Ö*'.
13. FM 3-09.70 p.I-20.
14. W. Schneider, '*Panzerhaubitze 2000: Entwicklung—Technik—Einsatz*' (2023), p.171.
15. Hunnicutt, '*Sheridan*', p.316–318.
16. Hunnicutt, '*Sheridan*', p.316–318.
17. Hunnicutt, '*Sheridan*', p.316–318.
18. TM 9-2350-311-10, p.2-152.
19. TM 9-2350-314-10, p.2-259.
20. O. Kozubenko, '*Ekipazh SAU M109: Radiyemo, koly dobre dopomagayemo nashym hloptsyam*' ArmyInform (2023): armyinform.com.ua/2023/07/15/ekipazh-sau-m109-radiyemo-koly-dobre-dopomagayemo-nashym-hlopczyam/

21. O!Nebylovych, '*Bakhmutskyi napryamok. 92 OSHBr*', YouTube (2023): youtu.be/42qly-Iv_2s

Chapter 4

1. Schneider, '*Panzerhaubitze 2000*', pp.12–16.
2. Schneider, '*Panzerhaubitze 2000*', pp.16–29.
3. Schneider, '*Panzerhaubitze 2000*', p.78.
4. Schneider, '*Panzerhaubitze 2000*', pp.220–226.
5. Schneider, '*Panzerhaubitze 2000*', pp.33–36.
6. Schneider, '*Panzerhaubitze 2000*', pp.100–101. Even faster reloads could be achieved using the optional 48V electrical system.
7. S. Ortac, et al., '*NABK Based Next Generation Ballistic Table Toolkit*', 23rd International Symposium on Ballistics (2007).
8. Schneider, '*Panzerhaubitze 2000*', pp.170–177.
9. Schneider, '*Panzerhaubitze 2000*', p.177.
10. Schneider, '*Panzerhaubitze 2000*', p.40.
11. Dutch PzH 2000s have a 7.62mm FN MAG instead of the MG3.
12. Unlike the MB 838, the MTU-88 1 is not multifuel capable.
13. Schneider, '*Panzerhaubitze 2000*', pp.44–47.
14. Defense Express, '*Ukrainian Artillerymen About PzH 2000: Vacuum Cleaner, Tender Electronics and the "Tenacious Enemy" of this Howitzer*' (2023): en.defence-ua.com/weapon_and_tech/ukrainian_artillerymen_about_pzh_2000_vacuum_cleaner_tender_electronics_and_the_tenacious_enemy_of_this_howitzer-6607.html
15. Schneider, '*Panzerhaubitze 2000*', pp.220–226.
16. Forecast International, '*Panzerhaubitze 2000 155 mm Self-Propelled Howitzer*', Military Vehicles Forecast (1999).
17. S. Yuferev, '*PzH 2000 — Odna iz luchshikh i samykh skorostrelnykh SAU mira*', TopWar (2012): topwar.ru/13920-pzh-2000-odna-iz-luchshih-i-samyh-skorostrelnyh-sau-mira
18. Säbelzahnmöwe, '*MRSI Fähigkeit erklärt - Interview mit dem Entwickler der PzH 2000*', YouTube (2022): youtu.be/MHWIdUc2vDc
19. K. Schuller and D. Pilar, '*Der dritte schuss*', FAZ (2024): faz.net/aktuell/politik/ukraine/ukraine-krieg-mit-einer-deutschen-haubitze-gegen-russland
20. United24, '*Battle for Bakhmut: German-made PzH 2000 and Soviet Pion 2S7 against Russian troops*', YouTube (2023): youtu.be/qAOQGnSGNEg
21. Defense Express, '*Ukrainian Artillerymen About PzH 2000*'.
22. Defense Express, '*Why Ukraine Did Not Finalize the Agreement for 1,000 PzH 2000 Howitzers: Three Potential Reasons*' (2023): en.defence-ua.com/analysis/why_ukraine_did_not_finalize_the_agreement_for_1000_pzh_2000_howitzers_three_potential_reasons-8569.html
23. D. DeMella, '*The Evolution of Artillery for Increased Effectiveness*' (2008), p.19.
24. Also known as the Cannon-Launched Guided Projectile (CLGP).
25. CIA, '*Soviet Artillery Precision-Guided Munitions: A Conventional Weapons Initiative*' (1986), pp.1–3.
26. GLR — Guided Long Range; BER — Ballistic Extended Range
27. Leonardo, '*VULCANO 155*' brochure (2021).
28. C. Gall and V. Golovin, '*Some U.S. Weapons Stymied by Russian Jamming in Ukraine*', New York Times: nytimes.com/2024/05/25/world/europe/us-weapons-russia-jamming-ukraine.html
29. BONUS — Bofors Nutating Shell; SMArt — *Suchzündermunition Artillerie* ('artillery sensor-fused munition').
30. BAE Systems, '*155mm BONUS Datasheet*' (2021).
31. General Dynamics Ordnance and Tactical Systems, '*SMArt 155*' brochure.
32. Defense Express, '*Important Advantage of SMArt 155 Artillery Munitions Proves it More Useful Than Excalibur or Vulcano*' (2024): en.defence-ua.com/weapon_and_tech/important_advantage_of_smart_155_artillery_munitions_proves_it_more_useful_than_excalibur_or_vulcan-10920.html
33. The Armourer's Bench, '*Top Attack 155 BONUS In Ukraine*' (2023): armourersbench.com/2023/01/06/top-attack-155-bonus-in-ukraine/
34. D. Rice, '*Cluster Munitions Have Changed the Course of the Ukraine War*' Small Wars Journal (2023): smallwarsjournal.com/2023/12/29/cluster-munitions-have-changed-course-ukraine-war/
35. J. Lukiv and D. Willis, '*Biden agrees to give Ukraine anti-personnel mines*', BBC (2024): bbc.com/news/articles/cx2d1lj3nwqo

Chapter 5

1. Sometimes rendered 'Artillery System of the 1990s'. It was also called 'Mallet' in Verolme's marketing material.
2. C. Foss, '*Vickers AS-90: a gunner's gun*', JDW No. 25 (1986), pp.1254–1256.
3. Forecast International, '*Artillery System 90 155 mm Self-Propelled Howitzer*', Military Vehicles Forecast (1999).
4. Lexicar Brasil, '*Verolme*' (2014): lexicarbrasil.com.br/verolme/
5. UK Parliament, '*Written evidence submitted by Mr David Lister and Mr Jason Barnes (AVF0003)*' (2020), p.6.
6. Although 'Braveheart' is often used to refer to all AS90s, strictly speaking, the name only refers to the export desert-adapted AS90 with ERO. See Forecast International, '*AS90*'.
7. Manson, '*Guns, Mortars and Rockets*', p.72.
8. S. Gourley, '*Fire for effect: Western developments in self-propelled artillery*'., Armada International (1990).
9. J. Spurný, '*AS-90 Braveheart in detail*' (2003), p.11.
10. Spurný, '*AS-90*', pp.36–39.
11. Selex ES, '*Selex ES sees export success in UAE, New Zealand, Poland: €11.5M for artillery pointing systems*' (2013): web.archive.org/web/20130607055616/http://www.selex-es.com/media/press-releases/2013/08-05-2013.aspx
12. Forecast International, '*Artillery System 90 155 mm Self-Propelled Howitzer*', Military Vehicles Forecast (1999).
13. D. Hay, '*AS-90 Mk.2 Walk Around*', Prime Portal (2008): primeportal.net/artillery/dan_hay/as90/
14. Gourley, '*Fire for effect*'.
15. Manson, '*Guns, Mortars and Rockets*', p.27.
16. United24, '*British AS-90 Shows of Awesome power on the Ukrainian Frontline. Day with 116th Mechanized Brigade*', YouTube (2024): youtu.be/PvL_N_yRgPU
17. C. Moore, '*The Self-propelled Party Bus*', Key Military (2022): keymilitary.com/article/self-propelled-party-bus
18. Horstman, '*Hydrogas*' brochure (2024).
19. Forecast International, '*AS90*'.
20. A. Kiński, '*Debiut Kraba*', NTW 7/2001 (2001), pp.9–15.
21. The name 'Braveheart' can be translated to '*Chrobry*' ('Brave') in Polish, and it is this name that is referenced in the Forecast International '*AS90*' article.
22. Though it is often referred to as 'AHS Krab', 'AHS' simply stands for '*armatohaubica samobieżna*' ('self-propelled howitzer'); '*Krab*' is its actual name.
23. Kiński, '*Debiut Kraba*'.
24. T. Kwasek, '*Nowe szaty Kraba*', NTW 9/2015 (2015), pp.16–24.
25. J. Palowski, '*Krab Howitzers to get Korean Chassis. PGZ Decision Ends the Crisis*'., (2014): defence24.com/industry/krab-howitzers-to-get-korean-chassis-pgz-decision-ends-the-crisis
26. Altair Agencja Lotnicza, '*e-RAPORT MSPO 1/2020 — Regina w kontrolowanym poślizgu*' (2020): altair.com.pl/e-report/view?article_id%3D1220
27. J. Sabak, '*Nowa amunicja dla Kraba przekroczyła planowany zasięg*', Defence24 (2015): defence24.pl/geopolityka/nowa-amunicja-dla-kraba-przekroczyla-planowany-zasieg
28. T. Kwasek, '*Huta Stalowa Wola – rok nowych wyzwań*', NTW 5/2018 (2018), pp.34–39.
29. N. Swietochowski and D. Rewak, '*"KRAB" – new capabilities of the Polish Armed Forces*', Scientific Journal of the Military University of Land Force Vol. 50 No. 2 (2018), pp.141–161.
30. Forces News, '*UK buys Archer Artillery System from Sweden to replace kit sent to Ukraine*' (2023): forcesnews.com/news/uk-buys-archer-artillery-system-sweden-replace-kit-sent-ukraine
31. V. Stolyarchuk and M. Chubayi, '*Ukrayinski voyiny rozpovily yak SAU Krab nyshhyt okupantiv*' (2022): armyinform.com.ua/2022/08/28/ukrayinski-voyiny-rozpovily-yak-sau-krab-nyshhyt-okupantiv/
32. Mi Ukrayina, '*TSE TREBA BACHYTY! Tretya SHTURMOVA pokazala UNIKALNI kadry roboty SAU AS-90 po pozytsiyakh RF*
33. V. Litvin, '*Polski remontnyky pokazaly, yak remontuyut ukrayinskiSAU Krab nepodalik vid liniyi frontu*', ArmyInform (2023): armyinform.com.ua/2023/08/09/polski-remontnyky-pokazaly-yak-remontuyut-ukrayinski-sau-krab-nepodalik-vid-liniyi-frontu/

34 G. Allison, 'Britain to purchase Boxer-based RCH 155 artillery systems', UK Defence Journal (2024): ukdefencejournal.org.uk/britain-to-purchase-boxer-based-rch155-artillery-systems/
35 J. Graf, 'More Krab Howitzers for the Armed Forces. PGZ President: "We need 11 years to develop a new APC" [Interview]', Defence24 (2024): defence24.com/industry/more-krab-howitzers-for-the-armed-forces-pgz-president-we-need-11-years-to-develop-a-new-apc-interview
36 M. Szopa, 'Poland Procures Korean MBTs, Aircraft, and Howitzers', Defence24 (2022): defence24.com/defence-policy/poland-procures-korean-mbts-aircraft-and-howitzers

Chapter 6

1 Forecast International, 'AU-F1 (155 GCT) 155mm Self-Propelled Howitzer', Ordnance & Munitions Forecast (2008).
2 Images Défense, 'Le canon de 155 mm tracté du GIAT'. (1985): imagesdefense.gouv.fr/fr/canon-de-155-tracte.html
3 Forecast International, '155 TR F1 155mm Howitzer', Ordnance & Munitions Forecast (2004).
4 Forecast International, '155 TR F1 155mm Howitzer', Ordnance & Munitions Forecast (2004).
5 P. Girard, 'Le CAESAR, ou la genèse atypique d'un matériel d'armament', Confédération Amicale des Ingénieurs de l'Armement (2023): caia.net/revue-auteurs-rubriques-numeros/article/le-caesar-ou-la-genese-atypique-d-un-materiel-d-armement/1191
6 It was originally abbreviated 'CESAR', but then changed to conform to the common spelling of 'Caesar'.
7 Girard, 'Le CAESAR'.
8 Girard, 'Le CAESAR'.
9 Girard, 'Le CAESAR'.
10 Danish MoD, 'Danish military support for Ukraine', fmn.dk/en/topics/operations/ongoing-operations/danish-military-support-for-ukraine/
11 Girard, 'Le CAESAR'.
12 SVP 7-(07)268, pp.6–7.
13 Nexter, 'CAESAR Artillery System', YouTube (2008): youtu.be/sh_6sJiQrr4
14 Renault Trucks Defense, 'Sherpa 5 Euro 4 Long Cab Wheelbase 4500 mm' (2006).
15 L. Lagneau, 'Artillerie: M. Macron annonce la livraison par la France de CAESAr à l'Ukraine', Opex360 (2022): opex360.com/2022/04/22/artillerie-m-macron-annonce-la-livraison-par-la-france-de-caesar-a-lukraine/
16 Ministère des Armées, 'Artillery coalition "helping Ukraine built its future artillery"' (2024): defense.gouv.fr/en/news/artillery-coalition-helping-ukraine-built-its-future-artillery
17 Defense Express, 'Pros and Cons of CAESAR Performance on Battlefields From Ukrainian Artillerymen and From Defense Ministry' (2023): en.defence-ua.com/weapon_and_tech/pros_and_cons_of_caesar_performance_on_battlefields_from_ukrainian_artillerymen_and_from_defense_ministry-9014.html
18 As reposted on 'Soldat Udachi' on Vkontakte: vk.com/wall-46943161_1616420
19 G. Alyokhin, 'Ukrainskiy izlom — V rezhime "odnovremennogo ognevogo naleta"' (2023).
20 United24, 'Swedish Archer FH77BW L52 Howitzer in the Donetsk Region. Sniper Artillery in Action', YouTube (2024): youtu.be/NbEvpXuNfCE
21 S. Vey, 'Kolesnaya samokhodnaya artilleriya', Army-Guide (2009): web.archive.org/web/20180821160545/http://www.army-guide.com/rus/article/article_1323.html
22 S. Kozatskyi, 'Bohdana ACS: Ukraine's Pursuit of Optimal Chassis or Artillery Build-Up?', Militarnyi (2024): mil.in.ua/en/articles/bohdana-acs-ukraine-s-pursuit-of-optimal-chassis-or-artillery-build-up/
23 B. Miroshnychenko, 'Bohynya viyny. Yak Ukrayina naroshchuye vyrobnytstvo SAU "Bohdana"', Ekonomichna Pravda (2023): epravda.com.ua/publications/2023/12/12/707553/
24 The various models are often popularly known as 'Bohdana 1.0/2.0/etc.', although the ZSU does not seem to have an official designation for these variants. For an identification guide, see: 'Jeff', 'Identified variants of the 2S22 Bohdana', Defense Archives (2024): defensearchives.com/news/identified-variants-of-the-2s22-bohdana/
25 Kozatskyi, 'Bohdana'.
26 R. Romaniuk, 'Persha bytva "Bohdany"'.
27 Defence Express, 'After Successful Purchase of the Bohdana Self-Propelled Howitzers, Denmark Order More Weapons from Ukrainian Enterprises' (2024): en.defence-ua.com/news/after_successful_purchase_of_the_bohdana_self_propelled_howitzers_denmark_order_more_weapons_from_ukrainian_enterprises-12021.html
28 Militarnyi, 'Ukraine Unveils Towed Bohdana Artillery System to Foreign Partners' (2024): mil.in.ua/en/news/ukraine-unveils-towed-bohdana-artillery-system-to-foreign-partners/
29 Miroshnychenko, 'Bohynya viyny'.

Chapter 7

1 The Iraqis considered Czechoslovak T-55s to be of a better build quality than Soviet ones. E. Hooton, T. Cooper, and F. Nadimi, 'The Iran-Iraq War Vol. 2: Desperate Days – The Battles for Southern Iraq 1982–1986' (2016), p.45.
2 S. Marx, 'The DANA/ZUZANA Czechoslovak SPG Family', The Tankograd Gazette No. 16 (2002), pp.4–20.
3 F. Korán and J. Horák, 'DANA ShKH vz.77 in detail' (2011), pp.2–5.
4 Trenčín and Dubnica nad Váhom are in what is today Slovakia. Tatra is based in Kopřivnice, today part of Czechia.
5 While 'Dana' is an acronym, and thus often spelled 'DANA', 'Ondava', 'Zuzana', and 'Dita' are not acronyms, even though they are often spelled in all capital letters. The author has chosen to keep them uncapitalised.
6 M. Barabanov, A. Lavrov, and V. Tseluiko, 'The Tanks of August' (2010), p.19.
7 Vojenské historické muzeum, '155 mm samohybná kanónová húfnica Ondava' (2015): ebadatelnavhm.vhu.sk/item/5/31
8 'ZUZANA 155 mm samohybná kanónová húbnica', Apológia Vol. 6 (1993), p.28.
9 R. Kment, '155 mm ShKH Zuzana 2', Obrana Vol. 5 (2010), pp.28–29.
10 Excalibur Army, 'Artillery Systems' catalogue, pp.3–8.
11 M. Hlavatý, 'SOV - 152 mm náboj nárazový trieštivotrhavý pre KH vz.37 a H vz.18/47', Valka.cz (2009): valka.cz/SOV-152-mm-naboj-narazovy-triestivotrhavy-pre-KH-vz-37-a-H-vz-18-47-t94532#353517
12 M. Smíšek, 'CZK - vz. 77 DANA (152mm samohybná kanónová houfnice)', Valka.cz (2015): valka.cz/CZK-vz-77-DANA-152mm-samohybna-kanonova-houfnice-t12305#534570
13 Retia, 'Dana M2': retia.eu/military-and-security-systems/installation-of-special-electronics/dana-m2/
14 Excalibur Army, 'EA 155 mm SPGH DITA - MRSI 3 rounds', YouTube (2023): youtu.be/7zS3Yl0hu7Y
15 Tatra Trucks, 'Performance & Data Sheets: Tatra Military Vehicles', pp.2–3.
16 Tatra gearboxes like the Tatra 10 have two modes (normal/reduced) in which the gears operate; thus, while the Tatra 10 technically has only five forward and one reverse gear, it has 10+2 speeds.
17 V. Shubets, and O. Moseyichenok, 'Na Rivnenshhyni prohodyat vyprobuvannya samohidnoyi haubytsi DANA-M2', ArmyInform (2021): armyinform.com.ua/2021/04/28/na-rivnenshhyni-prohodyat-vyprobuvannya-camohidnoyi-gaubyczi-dana-m2/
18 O. Mazepa, 'Frontovyy epizod artrozrakhunku "Dany": reportazh iz peredovoyi', ArmyInform (2023): armyinform.com.ua/2023/10/02/artrozrahunok-sau-dana-nyshhyt-voroga-na-fronti-reportazh-iz-peredovoyi/
19 O. Yakovenko, 'SAU Zuzana 2 slovachchyny vyyavylysya nenadiynymy dlya ZSU na poli boyu' URAUA (2024): uraua.info/2024/07/sau-zuzana-2-slovachchyny-vyyavylysya-nenadijnymy-dlya-zsu-na-poli-boyu/
20 56 Mech., '152-mm SPG "Dana-M2" In The Service With The 56th Mariupol Brigade.', YouTube (2024):
21 Azov, 'AZOV AND WESTERN WEAPONS. A cutting-edge SPGH in action against the occupiers [ENG]', YouTube (2024): youtu.be/EElDyzHJSs0
22 KNDS, 'KNDS offers the complete range of proven artillery systems' (2024): knds.fr/en/our-news/latest-news/knds-offers-complete-range-proven-artillery-systems
23 R. Lindström, and C.-G. Svantesson, 'Svensk teknik i världsklass', Militär Historia No. 10 (2013), pp.50–54.

24 M. Persson, '*15,5 cm haubitser*', Chalmers University of Technology: web.archive.org/web/20050227021820/http://www.mvs.chalmers.se/~m95perm_2/vapen/kanon/div/15.5cm_haub.html
25 J. Joseph, '*Arms and the Middlemen*', India Legal (2016): web.archive.org/web/20181025185933/http://www.indialegallive.com/viewpoint/arms-and-the-middlemen-14454
26 Persson, '*15,5 cm haubitser*'.
27 G. Persson and L. Björklund, '*Regeringens proposition 2005/06:132: Renovering och modifiering av artillerisystemet Haubits 77B*', Regeringskansliet (2005).
28 S. Bratt, '*Proposition om REMO av haubits 77*', Artilleri-Tidskrift No. 2 (2006), pp.30–32.
29 Försvarets materielverk, '*Bilaga 1 till årsredovisningen 2018, Uppföljning av pågående större anskaffningar*'' (2019), p.4.
30 BAE, '*ARCHER Mobile Howitzer 6x6*' brochure (2023).
31 SVT Nyheter, '*Svenska Archer på plats i Ukraina*' (2023): svt.se/nyheter/snabbkollen/svenska-archer-pa-plats-i-ukraina--ltds6g
32 Forces News, '*British Army's Archer arsenal now complete with the arrival of 10 more howitzers*' (2024): forcesnews.com/technology/weapons-and-kit/british-armys-archer-arsenal-now-complete-arrival-10-more-howitzers
33 Volvo Construction Equipment, '*Volvo A30E*': volvoce.com/global/en/products-and-services/past-products/articulated-haulers/volvo/a30e/
34 BAE, Archer brochure.
35 United24, '*Swedish Archer FH77BW L52 Howitzer in the Donetsk Region. Sniper Artillery in Action*', YouTube (2024): youtu.be/NbEvpXuNfCE
36 Persson & Björklund, '*Regeringens proposition 2005/06:132*'.

ABOUT THE AUTHOR

Wen-Jian Chung is a PhD student at the University of California, Irvine with a long-term interest in tank development, particularly Soviet, Russian and Ukrainian tanks. This is his fourth book for Helion.